Keep Going

Englisch für berufliche Schulen

4th edition

Vocabulary Practice Book

von
Steve Williams

in Zusammenarbeit
mit der Verlagsredaktion

Cornelsen

Projektleitung: Jim Austin
Verlagsredaktion: Kari-ann Seamark
Layout und technische Umsetzung: David van der Kemp, Berlin
Umschlaggestaltung: Klein & Halm Grafikdesign, Berlin

Erhältlich sind auch:

Schülerbuch	ISBN 978-3-06-024148-4
Workbook Wirtschaft mit Audio-CD	ISBN 978-3-06-024149-1
Workbook Technik mit Audio-CD	ISBN 978-3-06-450406-6
Workbook Soziales mit Audio-CD	ISBN 978-3-06-450421-9
Handreichungen zum Unterricht mit CD-ROM und 2 Audio-CDs	ISBN 978-3-06-024156-9

www.cornelsen.de

1. Auflage, 1. Druck 2010

Alle Drucke dieser Auflage sind inhaltlich unverändert
und können im Unterricht nebeneinander verwendet werden.

Druck: H. Heenemann, Berlin

ISBN 978-3-06-024184-2

Inhalt gedruckt auf säurefreiem Papier aus nachhaltiger Forstwirtschaft.

Inhalt

Let's go!

adult	This game is for adults only.	Erwachsene/r
adventure	The trip will be an adventure.	Abenteuer
advertisement	Here's an advertisement for a job.	Anzeige
to allow	I can't allow you to smoke here.	erlauben
at least	We need at least €100.	zumindest, wenigstens
to be allowed to	We aren't allowed to smoke.	dürfen
to beat (sb)	Germany beat England 2:0.	(jdn) schlagen
to build	They are building a house.	bauen
to call	Don't call me an idiot!	nennen
category	Which category: vegetable or fruit?	Kategorie
character	James Bond is a character, not a real person.	Charakter, (Film-, Roman-)Figur
clever	<> stupid	klug
company	BP is a large company.	Firma
complicated	The story is complicated.	kompliziert
to copy	Can I copy your work?	abschreiben, kopieren
creative	We need creative ideas.	kreativ
criminal	He's a criminal. Call the police.	Verbrecher/in
to design	She designs websites.	entwerfen, gestalten
electricity	Electricity is a sort of energy.	Elektrizität
extremely	= very	äußerst
favourite	Chips are my favourite food.	Lieblings-
finally	Finally, we went home.	zuletzt, endlich
(for) free	You can play for free.	gratis
gap	Write a word in the gap.	Lücke
gift	It's a birthday gift for you.	Geschenk
to grow	= to get larger	wachsen

to hurt oneself	Did you hurt yourself?	sich wehtun
industry	I work in the car industry.	Branche
information	I need more information.	Informationen
intelligence	Is IQ the same as intelligence?	Intelligenz
light	There isn't enough light in here.	Licht, Lampe
to mean	What does this word mean?	bedeuten
member	He's a member of the golf club.	Mitglied
not ... yet	I haven't done it yet. I'll do it now.	noch nicht
object	In English all objects are 'it'.	Gegenstand
phrase	'For free' is a phrase.	Formulierung
popular	He's popular at school.	beliebt
practical	We need practical suggestions.	praktisch
product	The company makes good products.	Produkt
professional	He's a professional musician.	Berufs-, professionell
to repair	I want to repair this bicycle.	reparieren
salespeople	The salespeople work in the shop.	Verkaufspersonal
skill	You need skill to win this game.	Fähigkeit, Fertigkeit
to sound	That sounds silly.	klingen
statement	Is it a statement or a question?	Aussage, Behauptung
strength	Sport improves your strength.	Stärke, Kraft
sure	I'm not sure if you're right.	sicher(lich)
to surprise sb	The answer surprised him.	jdn überraschen
to teach	Teach me to play tennis.	beibringen, lehren
technology	I love modern technology.	Technik, Technologie
tool	A hammer is a useful tool.	Werkzeug
training	You need training for this job.	Ausbildung
to translate	Translate this into German.	übersetzen

How much have you learned? Do the tasks to find out.
Only look at pages 4–5 if you are stuck.

1 **Find words that match the clues. The first letter is given to help you.**

1 This is a person who is no longer a teenager.

a ____________________

2 This is an organization which sells something.

c ____________________

3 If you are this, then you can make new things or have new ideas.

c ____________________

4 This is a group of words that belong together.

p ____________________

5 This is something a person has learned to do.

s ____________________

6 These are people who work in a shop.

s ____________________

7 If you have a lot of this, you can carry heavy things.

s ____________________

8 You use it to make things.

t ____________________

9 This helps you to do a new job.

t ____________________

10 It's a sort of energy. Computers and kitchen machines need it.

e ____________________

11 If your car doesn't work, ask someone to do this to it.

r ____________________

12 This will make your life more exciting.

a ____________________

13 He or she does something which is illegal.

c ____________________

14 This is a space where something should be.

g ____________________

2 **Work out the anagrams to complete the sentences.**

1 I love ice cream. It's my ______________________ TOFRIUVEA food.

2 Who can ______________________ TELRASNAT this sentence from English into German?

3 Look at this ______________________ TATESMIEVENRD. It says that the supermarket wants more shop assistants.

4 This question is really hard. You're very ______________________ LEVCER to find the answer so quickly.

5 It's a very ______________________ ROPLUAP TV show. Everyone in our class watches it.

6 It's our teacher's birthday tomorrow. Let's ______________________ SIRRUESP her with a nice present.

7 There is a lot of ______________________ TOFMINRONAI about new computer games on this website.

8 Do you think that new ______________________ LEOGYOCNHT can solve all the world's problems?

9 Our school is very old. It's time to ______________________ DUBLI a new one, I think.

10 I want a ______________________ TACLICAPR job. I want to work with my hands.

11 You don't need a question mark at the end of this sentence: it's a ______________________ SEMTETANT.

12 This machine is really ______________________ CATIMOCDLEP: there are a lot of different parts.

13 Today is an ______________________ LYMXETERE hot day – over 40°C.

14 Which ______________________ NUSDIRTY do you want to work in?

15 I like boxing. I would like to be a ______________________ RFSPOEIASNOL boxer when I'm older.

16 You can't come in here. It's only for ______________________ EBRMEMS.

17 My favourite ______________________ ACTHCRARE in the Simpsons is Homer.

UNIT 1 Fitness and sport

appointment	My appointment is with Ms Smith.	Termin
to belong to sb	Does this belong to you?	jdm gehören
carefully	Listen carefully!	sorgfältig
to check	Now check your work.	überprüfen
choice	There isn't a choice, we must do it.	Wahl, Auswahl
college	I'm going to college after school.	Berufsschule
competition	Our team won the competition.	Wettbewerb
conversation	Don't listen to our conversation.	Gespräch, Unterhaltung
current	Her current boyfriend is nice.	aktuell
daily routine	Exercise is part of my daily routine.	Tagesablauf
difference	What's the difference between them?	Unterschied
to discuss	Can we discuss this problem?	besprechen
drug	Cannabis is an illegal drug.	Droge
to enjoy sth	Do you enjoy swimming?	etw genießen, gern haben
equipment	How do I use this equipment?	Geräte, Ausrüstung
female	It's an all-female team: girls only.	weiblich
to fix sth	Can you fix my car?	etw reparieren
to follow	You have to follow the rules.	folgen
to get up	I get up at 6 o'clock.	aufstehen
gym	Arnold goes to the gym every day.	Fitness-Studio
healthy	Fruit is healthy, but chocolate isn't.	gesund
to hire sb	We need to hire three new people.	jdn einstellen
home	Everyone needs a home.	Zuhause
homeless	Many homeless people sleep in parks.	obdachlos
to improve	The weather is improving.	verbessern, (sich) bessern
independent	She's an independent person.	unabhängig

instructions	Read the instructions first.	Anleitung
to last	The film lasts 90 minutes.	dauern
to laugh	Don't laugh, it isn't funny.	lachen
leisure	= free time	Freizeit
to maintain	I maintain the computer system.	warten, unterhalten
male	It's an all-male team: no girls.	männlich
manager	The managers run the company.	Geschäftsführer/in, Leiter/in
meaning	What's the meaning of this word?	Bedeutung
opinion	In my opinion, you're wrong.	Meinung
overweight	I weigh 90 kilos. I'm overweight.	übergewichtig
possibility	There are two possibilities: left or right.	Möglichkeit
to report	Report to the class what you find out.	berichten
responsible	Who is responsible for cleaning?	zuständig
routine	He always follows the same routine.	Routine
to run sth	Mrs Patrick runs the centre.	etw betreiben, leiten
safe	<> dangerous	sicher
safety	Safety is important at work.	Sicherheit
several	There are several cars in the car park.	mehrere
sign	The sign says 'No smoking'.	Schild
skiing	We go skiing in the Alps.	Skifahren
soccer	BE: football	Fußball *(AE)*
staff	Ten staff work here.	Personal, Angestellte
to suit	Does Monday suit you?	passen
to supervise	Please supervise children in the pool.	beaufsichtigen
tall	She's 1.6 metres tall.	groß (Körpergröße)
task	I can't do this task. It's difficult.	Aufgabe
timetable	Which lesson is next in your timetable?	Stundenplan
trainee	The trainees work here for three years.	Auszubildende/r

How much have you learned? Do the tasks to find out.
Only look at pages 8–9 if you are stuck.

1 **Complete the crossword.**

1 When two or more people talk to each other, it's called a … .

2 … is another word for 'free time'.

3 If you're heavier than you should be, you are … .

4 Many people go to a … to become fit and strong.

5 Women and girls are … people.

6 Men and boys are … people.

7 Things you do every day are part of your daily … .

8 A … is someone who is learning to do a job.

9 … people don't have a place to live.

10 What you think about something is your … about it.

11 A … is a place where young people go for training.

12 … tell you how to do something.

2 **Find the vowels to complete the missing words.**

1 If you want to know the ______________________ MNNG of a word, look it up in a dictionary.

2 There isn't much ______________________ CHC in the college restaurant today. There's just pizza or pasta.

3 Don't shout at me. Why don't we ______________________ DSCSS this quietly?

4 Look at your ______________________ TMTBL to find out what lesson is next.

5 Can I speak to the person who is ______________________ RSPNSBL for hiring staff, please?

6 Don't go skiing unless you have the right ______________________ QPMNT.

7 Drive ______________________ CRFLLY in the wet weather.

8 I'm sorry. You can't see Ms Smith without an ______________________ PPNTMNT.

9 Anna is an ______________________ NDPNDNT person. She likes to do things her own way.

10 For a ______________________ HLTHY life, you need to eat well and get enough exercise.

11 ______________________ SFTY at work is very important. You don't want to hurt yourself or someone else, do you?

12 What's the most important ______________________ DFFRNC between colleges in England and in Germany?

13 You shouldn't ______________________ LGH at people who are less lucky than you.

14 There are ______________________ SVRL mistakes in this text. Can you find all of them?

15 My ______________________ CRRNT teacher is better than my teacher last year.

16 Our new ______________________ TRN is very clever. She learns quickly.

17 I don't have much ______________________ LSR time. I'm too busy.

18 That book ______________________ BLNGS to me. It's not yours.

UNIT 2 English around the world

abroad	He lives abroad, in France.	im Ausland
advice	I need advice about what to do.	Rat, Ratschläge
area	The park covers a large area.	Bereich, Gebiet
around	Around 3.5 million people live in Berlin.	ungefähr, zirka
to be able to	Are you able to help me?	in der Lage sein, können
brand	Nike is a famous brand.	Marke
can	A can of cola, please.	Dose
mobile phone	AE: cell phone	Handy *(BE)*
colleague	This is my colleague, Sue.	Kollege/Kollegin
to communicate	We communicate by email.	kommunizieren
contest	I won the contest.	Wettbewerb
countryside	The countryside is better than towns.	Landschaft, Land
customer	There are 10 customers in the shop.	Kunde/Kundin
disaster	Hurricane Katrina was a disaster.	Katastrophe
divorced	He's her ex-husband: they're divorced.	geschieden
driving licence	You can't drive without a driving licence.	Führerschein
engaged	We're engaged. We're getting married.	verlobt
event	A birthday is an important event.	Ereignis
exchange	I did an exchange with a British student.	Austausch, Tausch
exercise	You need more exercise.	Bewegung
to expect	I expect the train will come soon.	erwarten
experience	My holiday was an interesting experience.	Erfahrung, Erlebnis
farmer	We need farmers to grow our food.	Landwirt/in
to feel homesick	I feel homesick. I want to go home.	Heimweh haben
to fight	Children! Don't fight in the car!	(be)kämpfen, streiten
foreign	⚠ Aussprache	fremd
foreigner	I'm not a foreigner, I was born here.	Ausländer/in

to get exercise	I get exercise every day.	Sport treiben
government	The government runs the country.	Regierung
to guess	Can you guess the answer?	raten, erraten
health	Her health is good. She's never ill.	Gesundheit
homesickness	I get homesickness when I'm away.	Heimweh
internship	I'm doing an internship in a company.	Praktikum
to invite	I invited 50 guests to my party.	einladen
key	I can't find the key to the door.	Schlüssel
to marry	I can't marry you: I've got a wife.	heiraten
to mention	You didn't mention your name.	erwähnen, (be)nennen
menu	There's pizza and pasta on the menu.	Speisekarte
to miss sb/sth	He misses his family when he's away.	jdn/etw vermissen
to name	They named their son Jim	benennen, nennen
to photograph	He photographs rock stars.	fotografieren
photograph	That's me in the photograph.	Foto(grafie)
to promise	I promise to love you for ever.	versprechen
to serve	Can you serve me, please?	servieren
similar	It isn't the same, but it's similar.	ähnlich
soldier	He is a soldier in the US army.	Soldat/in
special	A birthday is a special day.	besonders, Spezial-
strange	You won't believe it, it's a strange story.	seltsam, komisch
subject	I don't want to talk about that subject.	Thema
sure	I'm not sure this is right.	sicher
technician	She works as a technician.	Techniker/in
terrible	I have a terrible headache.	furchtbar, schrecklich
title	What's the title of that book?	Titel
translation	Do a translation from English to German.	Übersetzung
vegetarian	Vegetarians don't eat meat.	Vegetarier/in

How much have you learned? Do the tasks to find out.
Only look at pages 12–13 if you are stuck.

1 **Work out the anagrams. Then complete the puzzle to find a group that helps people in different countries around the world.**

a) I'd like to work DABRAO – in the USA perhaps.
☐☐☐☐☐☐ (21, 15, 1)

b) How many GEFRION languages do you speak?
☐☐☐☐☐☐☐ (14, 24, 16, 2, 25)

c) The RETNEOVMGN should do something about this problem. They shouldn't leave it to ordinary people like us.
☐☐☐☐☐☐☐☐☐☐ (19, 6)

d) There are SEROLDIS from many countries in Afghanistan.
☐☐☐☐☐☐☐☐ (5, 11)

e) Many people have problems with KEHCEISNMOSS when they're away from home.
☐☐☐☐☐☐☐☐☐☐☐☐ (20, 10)

f) The tsunami was a terrible STADISER. Many people died.
☐☐☐☐☐☐☐☐ (4)

g) In poor countries like Ethiopia, many people's LETHAH is bad.
☐☐☐☐☐☐ (7, 18, 22)

h) Here is a ROPHAOPGHT of my family in Iran.
☐☐☐☐☐☐☐☐☐☐ (8)

i) The SNIANIHCETC install wind turbines to give poor villages electricity.
☐☐☐☐☐☐☐☐☐☐☐ (12, 23)

j) I'm doing an NECXHGAE with an Irish boy this year.
☐☐☐☐☐☐☐☐ (17, 13)

k) Spending a month in India will be an interesting REECEPNIXE for you.
☐☐☐☐☐☐☐☐☐☐ (9)

l) I hope to get a six-month SIPNITRHEN with a company in Italy.
☐☐☐☐☐☐☐☐☐☐ (3)

1	2	3	4	5	6	7	8	-	9	10	11	12	13	14		15	16	17	18	19	20	Z	21	22	23	24	25

2 **Complete the sentences with the English translations of the words in brackets.**

1 Ben is fat because he doesn't get enough ______________________. (*Bewegung*)

2 I ______________________ it will rain later. (*erwarten*)

3 There are a lot of ______________________ in the shop. (*Kunden/Kundinnen*)

4 Did Emma ______________________ you to her party? (*einladen*)

5 Can you ______________________ how much money I have in my pocket? (*erraten*)

6 My T-shirt isn't the same as yours, but it's ______________________. (*ähnlich*)

7 Most of the ______________________ in this town are tourists. (*Ausländer/innen*)

8 Do you ______________________ your friends when you go on holiday? (*vermissen*)

9 Are you ______________________ this is the right answer? (*sicher*)

10 That book looks interesting. What's the ______________________? (*Thema*)

11 Are the ______________________ in your office nice? (*Kollegen/Kolleginnen*)

12 You can't drive a car without a ______________________ ______________________. (*Führerschein*)

13 Can we have the ______________________, please? (*Speisekarte*)

14 Your sunglasses are really cool! What ______________________ are they? (*Marke*)

3 **Circle the correct word to complete the sentences.**

1 Ann and Jason are *engaged / divorced*. They will get married next year.

2 I didn't know the answer so I *expected / guessed*.

3 I need some *advice / exercise*. I don't know how to stop feeling homesick.

4 She's a *technician / vegetarian* so she doesn't eat meat.

5 I would like to do an *exchange / internship*. I would like to stay with a family in America and go to school there for a year.

6 Going to school in England was a good *event / experience* for me.

7 The party was a *disaster / contest*. Everything went wrong!

8 That could be the answer but I'm not *sure / special*.

UNIT 3 Free-time activities

accommodation	What accommodation do you have – a hotel?	Unterkunft
to apply	I want to apply for this job.	sich bewerben
to attend sth	20,000 people attended the festival.	in/zu etw gehen
available	Sorry, that book isn't available any longer.	erhältlich
to camp	They camped in a field.	zelten
campsite	They stayed on a campsite in Italy.	Campingplatz
cash	I don't have any cash, just my credit card.	Bargeld
caterer	The caterers are working in the kitchen.	Lieferant von Speisen und Getränken
to chat	Stop chatting and get on with your work!	sich unterhalten
to climb	Don't climb that tree: it's dangerous.	klettern
curriculum vitae (CV)	AE: résumé	Lebenslauf *(BE)*
disabled	Where are the disabled toilets?	behindert, Behinderten-
education	You need a good education to get a good job.	(Schul-)Bildung
entertainment	He works in entertainment. He's a TV star.	Unterhaltung
entry	How much does entry to the disco cost?	Eintritt, Zutritt
event	He works at concerts and other events.	Veranstaltung
fence	There's a fence between the two gardens.	Zaun
to fit (sth)	It won't fit in my bag. It's too big.	(zu/in etw) passen
fluent	His mum is French so his French is fluent.	fließend
ground	The apples fell to the ground.	Boden, Erde
to include	We all need to work. That includes you, Jo.	beinhalten, umfassen
kind	What kind of food do you like best?	Art
to look sth up	He didn't know the word, so he looked it up.	etw (im Wörterbuch) nachschlagen
meal	I eat three meals a day.	Essen, Mahlzeit
musician	She's a musician. She plays the piano.	Musiker/in

nearby	There isn't a shop nearby.	in der Nähe
paramedic	He's very ill. We need a paramedic.	Sanitäter/in
payment	He made a payment of fifty euros.	Zahlung
piano	I'd like to play the piano.	Klavier
pie	This apple pie is still hot.	Kuchen, Pastete
pleased	I'm pleased with the photo: it's good.	froh, erfreut
poster	The concert information is on the poster.	Plakat
primary school	Ben started primary school at the age of five.	Grundschule
to put sth up	They put up signs saying 'No parking'.	etw aufstellen
reference	We need a reference from your last employer.	Referenz
retail	I work in retail, in a shop.	Einzelhandel
sales	If you want to buy it, ask the sales assistant.	Verkauf, Vertrieb
secondary school	At 11 he went to secondary school.	weiterführende Schule
security officer	The security officer is important for safety.	Sicherheits-bedienstete/r
to sign	Don't forget to sign the letter.	unterschreiben
situation	⚠ Aussprache	Situation
to solve	Who can solve this problem for me?	lösen
stage	The rock star is on the stage.	Bühne
stuff	Who put all this stuff here?	Zeug, Kram
style	I like all styles of music: indie, techno, R & B.	Stil
survey	I'm doing a survey. Can I ask a question?	Umfrage, Erhebung
tent	When we go camping we stay in a tent.	Zelt
truck	Put all the boxes on the truck.	Lastwagen
urgent	Phone the police quickly. It's urgent.	dringend
voluntary	I don't get paid: it's a voluntary job.	freiwillig, ehrenamtlich
volunteer	I work for free. I'm a volunteer, you see.	Freiwillige/r
work placement	Three students are doing work placements.	Praktikum
worth	It's only a T-shirt. It isn't worth €100.	wert, im Wert von

How much have you learned? Do the tasks to find out.
Only look at pages 16–17 if you are stuck.

1 **Find the other part of each word in the box and then write its German meaning.**

ano • by • clude • commodation • ed • end •
ent • ent • ~~er~~ • ian • ion • mary • medic • ment •
ment • ply • site • tail • tary • very

1 poster______ Plakat______
2 flu______ ______
3 urg______ ______
4 music______ ______
5 educat______ ______
6 entertain______ ______
7 ap______ ______
8 ac______ ______
9 in______ ______
10 volun______ ______
11 near______ ______
12 pay______ ______
13 re______ ______
14 para______ ______
15 disabl______ ______
16 att______ ______
17 camp______ ______
18 sur______ ______
19 pi______ ______
20 pri______ ______

2 **Read the clues, then find the words in the word square. There are five letters left over. Can you use them to spell the name of a musical instrument?**

1 It keeps people or animals in or out.

____

2 You might do this on holiday instead of staying in a hotel.

____

3 Money in the form of notes and coins.

____

4 Most people eat three of these a day.

____

5 Friends like to do this on the phone.

____

6 It's another word for 'things'.

____

7 This is where you'll find the band at a concert.

____

8 If you're sleeping in one of these, you don't want cold, windy weather.

____

9 If you're clever, you can do this to a problem.

____

10 Don't forget to do this if you write a letter.

____

P	S	O	L	V	E	I
N	S	I	G	N	C	S
F	C	H	A	T	A	T
E	M	E	A	L	M	U
N	C	A	S	H	P	F
C	A	T	E	N	T	F
E	O	S	T	A	G	E

The musical instrument is a ______________________ .

UNIT 4 Life in the big city

accident	Drive carefully, or you'll have an accident.	Unfall
appetizer	I'll start with an appetizer, please.	Appetithappen
to argue	Don't argue with me! You're wrong!	sich streiten
average	The average age in this class is 16.	Durchschnitt(s-)
bill	'Anything else, sir?' – 'Just the bill, please.'	Rechnung
block of flats	He lives on the 14th floor of a block of flats.	Wohnblock, Mietshaus
to borrow	You can borrow my dress for the party.	ausleihen
building	A house is a type of building.	Gebäude
chef	He works as a chef in a restaurant.	Koch/Köchin
contact lens	I don't need glasses, I wear contact lenses.	Kontaktlinse
cook	Five cooks work in the restaurant.	Koch/Köchin
to deliver	Can you deliver it to 13 Crown Road, please?	liefern, anliefern
delivery	Here's a pizza delivery for Mr Benn.	Lieferung
dessert	What's for dessert? Ice cream?	Nachtisch, Dessert
direction	Which direction? Left or right?	Richtung
dish, dishes	Spaghetti is his favourite dish.	Gericht, Geschirr
to get around	She uses a moped to get around.	herumkommen
to get to know sb	It took us years to get to know them.	jdn kennen lernen
to give sb directions	Could you give me directions to the post office, please?	jdm den Weg zeigen
guide	A guide showed us the tourist attractions.	Führer
huge	It's a huge city, much bigger than Berlin.	riesig, groß
ID	Can I see your ID, please?	Ausweis
to imagine	Imagine if we could fly.	sich vorstellen
immediately	Eat it immediately, while it's hot.	sofort, unverzüglich
ingredient	The ingredients include eggs, water, ...	Zutat
instead	There are no chips. Is salad okay instead?	stattdessen

main dish	I'll have fish for my main dish.	Hauptgericht
to miss sth	We've missed it. We have to go back.	etw verfehlen
noisy	It's so noisy here – my ears hurt!	laut, lärmend
opposite	Black is the opposite of white.	Gegenteil
to order	Waiter! We're ready to order, please.	bestellen
pharmacy	I need some pills from the pharmacy.	Apotheke
platform	The train to Reading leaves from platform 1.	Bahnsteig
population	The population is about 100 million.	Bevölkerung
to prepare	How do you prepare this fish?	zubereiten
to produce	The farm produces chickens and eggs.	produzieren, herstellen
relaxed	I'm feeling relaxed: it will be OK.	locker, entspannt
reservation	I'd like to make a reservation, please.	Reservierung
to ride sth	I ride my bike to work.	etw fahren
screen	Read the email on the screen, don't print it.	Bildschirm
seafood	Seafood includes fish and shellfish.	Meeresfrüchte
separate	Can we have three separate bills, please?	getrennt
single room	I only need a single room: there's just me.	Einzelzimmer
stadium	The football match is in the stadium.	Stadion
stressed out	It's busy, so we're all stressed out.	gestresst
strict	Our teacher is strict: we have to work hard.	streng
to taste	Mmm! This steak tastes good.	schmecken
temperature	⚠ Aussprache	Temperatur
to throw sth away	Throw this old bread away, please.	etw wegwerfen
tiny	It's very small – tiny, in fact.	winzig, klein
traffic	There's a lot of traffic on the roads today.	Verkehr
to train	Josh trained as a music teacher.	eine Ausbildung machen
underground	AE: subway	U-Bahn *(BE)*
upstairs	The bedrooms are upstairs, not down here.	oben

How much have you learned? Do the tasks to find out.
Only look at pages 20–21 if you are stuck.

1 **Find the following words in the word snake. Write the German meaning next to each word.**

TASTESEAFOODORDERINGREDIENTDISHESDESSERTCOOKCHEFBILLAPPETIZER

Eight nouns to do with restaurants and food:

Two verbs to do with restaurants and food:

2 Complete the crossword.

1 Gebäude
2 ausleihen
3 Richtung
4 Verkehr
5 eine Ausbildung machen
6 Gegenteil
7 Ausweis
8 Unfall
9 Durchschnitt
10 stattdessen
11 Bildschirm
12 Reservierung

3 Match the words which go together.

1 get	a away
2 get	b around
3 give	c to know
4 contact	d room
5 single	e directions
6 throw	f lens

UNIT 5 The world in 2050

ability	An ability to listen is important in this job.	Fähigkeit
to agree	I agree: you're right.	zustimmen
angry	Don't get angry with me: it isn't my fault.	wütend, verärgert
to be addictive	Cigarettes are addictive.	süchtig machen
career	It's a job, but is it really a career for life?	Karriere, Beruf
charity	The Red Cross and Oxfam are large charities.	gemeinnützige Organisation
climate change	How can we stop climate change?	Klimawandel
to compare	Compare the two cars: which one is faster?	vergleichen
creativity	Creativity is useful in a lot of media jobs.	Kreativität
definitely	It's definitely the best thing to do.	bestimmt, absolut
depressing	This film is depressing. Please turn it off.	deprimierend
to disagree	I disagree: you're wrong.	nicht zustimmen
duty	It's your duty to help these people.	Aufgabe, Pflicht
employee	The company has 50 employees.	Angestellte/r
to express	I'm only expressing my opinion.	ausdrücken
hopefully	Hopefully I'll pass my exams.	hoffentlich
human	The first human landed on the moon in 1969.	Mensch
imagination	Book writers need a lot of imagination.	Phantasie
imaginative	It's so imaginative. How did you think of it?	phantasievoll, kreativ
income	He lives on a low income: €20 a day.	Einkommen
to invent	Charles Babbage invented the first computer.	erfinden
invention	The internet is a very important invention.	Erfindung
lifetime	What events will we see in our lifetime?	Leben, Lebensdauer
to look after sb	Can you look after the baby for me?	sich um jdn kümmern
managing director	The managing director runs the company.	Geschäftsführer/in

message	Did you get my message about the party?	Mitteilung, Botschaft
on average	On average, women live longer than men.	durchschnittlich
optimistic	I'm optimistic. I think everything will be OK.	optimistisch
to organize	You need to organize your work better.	organisieren
particularly	AIDS is a big problem, particularly in Africa.	besonders
pensioner	Most people over 65 are pensioners.	Rentner/in
pollution	Cars cause a lot of pollution in our cities.	(Umwelt-)Verschmutzung
power	Computers need power to run.	*hier:* Energie, Strom
prediction	Make predictions about what will happen.	Voraussage
press	I don't believe everything I read in the press.	Presse
programme	There was an interesting programme on TV.	Sendung
realistic	The picture isn't realistic: it doesn't look like me.	realistisch, wirklichkeitsnah
reason	What's the reason for the changes?	Grund, Begründung
responsible	She's very responsible. She always does a good job.	verantwortungsbewusst, zuständig
result	My exam results were very good.	Ergebnis
risk	There is a risk that you might get hurt.	Risiko
self-confident	He's very self-confident. He thinks he's great.	selbstbewusst
serious	Don't laugh! It's a serious problem.	ernst, ernsthaft
speech	The minister gave a long and boring speech.	Rede; gesprochene Sprache
thought	I write my thoughts in my diary every day.	Gedanke
trip	We're going on a two-week trip to Paris.	Ausflug
to turn out	Everything turned out well in the end.	sich herausstellen
unemployment	Unemployment is when people lose jobs.	Arbeitslosigkeit
unnecessary	It's unnecessary: you don't need it.	unnötig
view	What's your view about it?	Ansicht
waste	Don't do it. It's a waste of time.	Verschwendung
wasteful	It's wasteful to throw old clothes away.	verschwenderisch
wealthy	I have a bit of money, but I'm not wealthy.	wohlhabend, reich

How much have you learned? Do the tasks to find out.
Only look at pages 24–25 if you are stuck.

1 **Complete the sentences with the noun form of the underlined words.**

1 He's able to play football really well: he shows a lot of ability.

2 It's a creative idea: it shows a lot of ____________________.

3 Can you imagine what will happen next? You don't need a lot of ____________________ for that.

4 He invented it: it's his ____________________.

5 You have to speak for 30 minutes: that's a long ____________________.

6 What do you think? You never tell me your ____________________s.

7 This company is wasteful: there's too much ____________________ here.

2 **All of the missing words have at least one pair of double letters. Complete the words.**

1 This is a really good book. Don't you _ _ _ EE?

2 Many illegal drugs are _ DD _ _ _ _ _ _.

3 Do you already have plans for your _ _ _ EE _ after you leave school?

4 I don't like that band. Their music is so _ _ _ _ _ SS _ _ _ – it makes me feel really down.

5 That's my opinion. I'm sorry that you _ _ _ _ _ _ EE with me.

6 Are you good enough to be an _ _ _ _ _ _ EE in our company?

7 _ _ _ _ _ _ LL _ my football team will win.

8 I left a _ _ SS _ _ _ for you about the party. Didn't you get it?

9 There aren't any fish in the water. There's too much _ _ LL _ _ _ _ _, you see.

10 It's a big scandal. There are a lot of stories in the _ _ _ SS about it.

11 Did you watch that _ _ _ _ _ _ MM _ about climate change on TV?

12 It's _ NN _ _ _ SS _ _ _ to shout. I can hear you if you talk normally.

3 **Find the vowels to complete the missing words.**

1 He/She is a person who doesn't work any more.

PNSNR ______________________

2 This is something you think will happen.

PRDCTN ______________________

3 This is why something happens.

RSN ______________________

4 It's the opposite of funny.

SRS ______________________

5 If you have a lot of money, this is what you are.

WLTHY ______________________

6 We only have one each.

LFTM ______________________

7 When you look at things to see what's the same and what's different, you're doing this.

CMPR ______________________

8 When people don't have jobs, there's a lot of this.

NMPLYMNT ______________________

9 It's another word for opinion.

VW ______________________

10 I'm one, and so are you.

HMN ______________________

11 A person who is this thinks that everything will turn out well.

PTMSTC ______________________

12 These organizations give help to people who need it.

CHRTY ______________________

13 You do this when you give your opinion.

XPRSS ______________________

14 This is how much money you get from your job.

NCM ______________________

UNIT 6 Social networks

accidentally	We weren't fighting: I hit him accidentally.	versehentlich, zufällig
to add	How can I add photos to my Facebook page?	hinzufügen
to advise	What do you advise me to do?	beraten, raten
to apologize	Don't apologize, it's OK.	sich entschuldigen
to attach	I forgot to attach the photos to the email.	beifügen, anhängen
to be embarrassed	He was embarrassed when he fell over.	sich schämen
behaviour	Your behaviour in class is a problem.	Verhalten, Benehmen
to break	Don't break the rules, or you're out.	brechen
by mistake	I sent it to the wrong person by mistake.	irrtümlich
clothing	= clothes	Kleidung
comment	The teacher wrote a comment in my book.	Bemerkung, Kommentar
common	Smith is a common surname.	häufig, weit verbreitet
to complain	If you don't like it, complain to the chef.	sich beschweren
complaint	I made a complaint about the bad food.	Beschwerde
criticism	I accept your criticism: I was wrong.	Kritik
to criticize	Don't criticize me! You're wrong.	kritisieren
to delete	Delete these old emails. We don't need them.	löschen
department	There are five departments in the company.	Abteilung
to embarrass sb	Mum! Don't embarrass me in front of my girlfriend!	jdm peinlich sein, jdn bloßstellen
embarrassment	I can see his embarrassment. His face is red.	Verlegenheit, Peinlichkeit
employer	He's my employer. I work for him.	Arbeitgeber/in
excellent	= very good	hervorragend
explanation	What's your explanation for this mistake?	Erklärung
face-to-face	Don't phone him. Talk to him face-to-face.	persönlich
feeling	He lost all feeling in his arm.	Gefühl

file	There are 2,500,000 files on your computer.	Datei
to forward	I need that email. Please forward it to me.	weiterleiten
to hurt	Ouch! I've hurt my head!	verletzen
informal	It's just an informal chat, not an interview.	informell
invitation	Did you get an invitation to the party?	Einladung
to keep in touch	Keep in touch when you're in the USA.	in Kontakt bleiben
to look forward to sth	I'm looking forward to the party next week.	sich auf etw freuen
to make sense	It doesn't make sense. What's its meaning?	Sinn ergeben
network	The internet is a computer network.	Netzwerk
noticeboard	He put my photo on the school noticeboard.	Pinnwand
occasionally	I don't eat chips often, only occasionally.	gelegentlich, hin und wieder
to offend	You've offended her. You must say sorry.	beleidigen
order	Put the letters in order to make a word.	Reihenfolge
potential	⚠ Aussprache	Potential
to quit	I don't like this job. I quit!	aufhören, aussteigen
to receive	I've just received this fax from Joe Davies.	erhalten
recipient	She sent the same email to 40 recipients.	Empfänger/in
to recognize	Oh, it's you! I didn't recognize you.	erkennen
to replace	If you lose your ticket, we can't replace it.	ersetzen, austauschen
to respect	You must respect your teachers.	achten, respektieren
rude	<> polite	unverschämt
shy	Don't be shy! Come over here and say hello.	schüchtern
suitable	Jeans aren't suitable for the office, Ms Smith.	passend
text message	Use your phone to send her a text message.	SMS
unfortunately	Unfortunately the weather was bad.	leider, unglücklicherweise
to update	You must update the letter before you send it.	aktualisieren
upset	Don't get upset! Everybody makes mistakes.	aufgeregt, verärgert
voice	Belinda has a very loud voice.	Stimme

How much have you learned? Do the tasks to find out.
Only look at pages 28–29 if you are stuck.

1 **Read the clues and complete the words.**

1 This is something you might say or write.
co______________

2 A person who feels this emotion might have a red face.
em______________

3 This is what you give to show why something happened.
ex______________

4 If you lose something, you may need to do this.
re______________

5 When you're this, you might cry or shout.
up______________

6 When you give something, this is the person who gets it.
re______________

7 If you don't need a file or email, you can do this to it.
de______________

8 A person who is angry about something might do this.
co______________

9 This is what the teacher says when your work is very good.
ex______________

10 It's nice to get one of these.
in______________

11 This happens when you see someone and think 'I know this person.'
re______________

12 When you tell someone what they should do, this is what you are doing.
ad______________

13 If an event is this, you don't need to wear smart clothes.
in______________

14 This is what you do when you add new information to a text.
up______________

15 When you get a job, this is the person you'll work for.
em______________

2 **Find the following words in the word square. Write the German meaning next to each word.**

Three nouns to do with communication:

______________________ ______________________

______________________ ______________________

______________________ ______________________

Three verbs you can do to an email:

______________________ ______________________

______________________ ______________________

______________________ ______________________

Five verbs you can do to a person by sending an email:

______________________ ______________________

______________________ ______________________

______________________ ______________________

______________________ ______________________

______________________ ______________________

N	E	T	W	O	R	K	A	J	A	V
O	F	A	Z	E	O	O	D	S	H	O
T	O	P	U	A	W	H	F	W	H	I
I	F	O	R	W	A	R	D	Y	U	C
C	F	L	U	O	T	E	N	A	R	E
E	E	O	V	G	T	R	E	O	T	A
B	N	G	A	R	A	E	J	I	G	R
O	D	I	R	E	C	E	I	V	E	K
A	R	Z	O	A	H	E	E	R	E	S
R	L	E	M	B	A	R	R	A	S	S
D	C	R	I	T	I	C	I	Z	E	P

UNIT 7 Future jobs and training

apprenticeship	Your apprenticeship will last three years.	Ausbildung(splatz)
awful	The film wasn't just bad, it was awful.	schrecklich, fürchterlich
button	Press this button to start the machine.	Knopf
carefully	Read it carefully so you don't miss anything.	*hier:* aufmerksam
certain	You may be right, but I'm not certain.	sicher
challenging	It's a challenging job: it won't be easy.	anspruchsvoll
classmate	Sue and her classmates have exams soon.	Klassenkamerad/in
construction	I work in construction: I like building things.	Baugewerbe
decision	Yes or no? It's your decision.	Entscheidung
to employ	Our business employs 2,500 people.	beschäftigen, einstellen
engineer	These engineers designed the bridge.	Ingenieur/in
enthusiastic	Not again! – Try and be more enthusiastic!	begeistert
to escape	They ran inside to escape the rain.	entkommen
to evaluate	How do you evaluate the situation?	bewerten, beurteilen
to fail	He lost everything when his business failed.	versagen, scheitern
fishing	He likes fishing but he doesn't eat fish.	Angeln
to get a haircut	Your hair is too long. Get a haircut.	sich die Haare schneiden lassen
heating	It's cold. Maybe the heating doesn't work.	Heizung
to install	Did you install the computer software?	installieren
interview	I have to go for an interview on Tuesday.	Vorstellungsgespräch
job interview	He went for a job interview at the company.	Vorstellungsgespräch
job-seeker	Are you a job-seeker or still at school?	Arbeitssuchende/r
knowledge	I don't have much knowledge of computers.	Wissen, Kenntnisse
lighting	It's too dark. We need better lighting.	Beleuchtung
machinery	JCB makes earth-moving machinery.	Maschinen
machinist	A machinist uses a machine to make parts.	Maschinist/in
to make sth up	It isn't true. You made it up!	sich etw ausdenken

management	The management wants us to work longer.	Geschäftsführung, Verwaltung
manufacturing	VW is a car manufacturing company.	Fertigung(sindustrie)
nasty	I'm not stupid: that was a nasty thing to say.	gemein
necessary	I don't enjoy doing it, but it's necessary.	nötig, notwendig
to operate	How do I operate this machine?	bedienen
out of date	The software is out of date. It's really slow.	überholt, veraltet
part-time	I only work part-time: 20 hours a week.	Teilzeit-
pay	Your pay will be €600 a week.	Lohn, Gehalt
position	You're the best person for this position.	Stelle, Position
power tool	Many power tools have batteries these days.	Elektrowerkzeug
to predict	Can you predict what will happen next?	voraussagen, vorhersehen
promotion	We're going to give you a promotion.	Beförderung
range	There is a range of magazines in the shop.	Reihe, Auswahl
reaction	What was his reaction to the news?	Reaktion
to reject	They rejected the idea because it was silly.	ablehnen
relevant	Is that relevant? Please explain.	relevant, wichtig
to require	This software requires Windows 7 or later.	erfordern, brauchen
responsibility	It's your responsibility to get there on time.	Verantwortung
sales assistant	= shop assistant	Verkäufer/in
school leaver	Many school leavers start their first job soon.	Schulabgänger/in
to succeed	If you don't try, you won't succeed.	gelingen, Erfolg haben
to suggest	I suggest that we have coffee now.	vorschlagen
suggestion	What do we do now? Any suggestions?	Vorschlag
traineeship	After college I did a traineeship in industry.	Ausbildungsplatz
transport	The transport minister wants more roads.	Verkehrswesen
unlikely	It may happen, but it's unlikely.	unwahrscheinlich
varied	They're varied, not all the same.	abwechslungsreich
vehicle	Cars, trains and motorbikes are vehicles.	Fahrzeug
to work out	Can you work out the answer?	herausfinden

How much have you learned? Do the tasks to find out.
Only look at pages 32–33 if you are stuck.

1 **Work out the anagrams and complete the grid to find out what industry Amy wants to work in.**

Amy wants to operate heavy (1) CYENRAHMI like big trucks or tractors. She hopes that a company will (2) MYLEPO her as a trainee when she finishes school. One company has already invited her for an (3) VEWITENRI. Her (4) SLEMACSAST at school think that Amy's choice of job is unusual for a girl. They say that she won't have much chance of (5) NOPTIORMO to a job with more responsibility. Amy's dad is an (6) NEEGINRE and works on large building projects. He wants her to think about her career (7) LALREFCYU.

Because Amy is interested in large (8) IVCEESHL like trucks, her brother thinks that she should get a traineeship in (9) NIFMUCGRANTUA. In the end though, it's Amy's own (10) COESINDI. She has a good (11) LOKEGNEWD of the industry she wants to work in. Hopefully she will get a (12) INISOOPT with a suitable company.

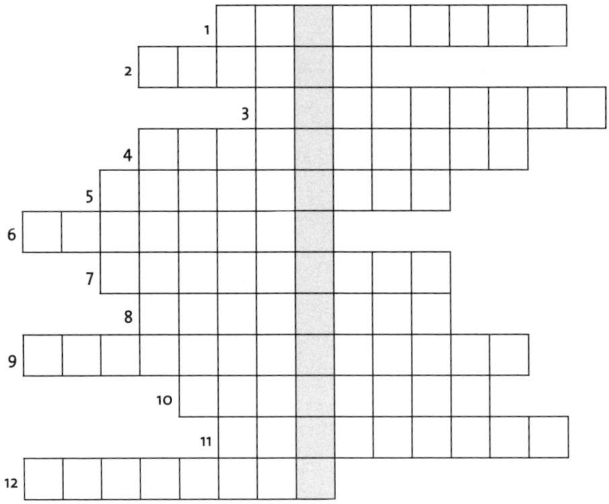

Amy's choice of industry: ______________________________

2 **Complete the sentences with the English translations of the words in brackets.**

1 He starts his ______________________ soon. (*Ausbildung*)

2 The red ______________________ stops the motor. (*Knopf*)

3 You're ______________________ to ______________________ if you try hard enough. (*sicher, Erfolg haben*)

4 On this course, you'll learn how to ______________________ heating systems. (*installieren*)

5 There are two million ______________________ in Germany at the moment. (*Arbeitssuchende*)

6 A good level of English is ______________________ in this job. (*notwendig*)

7 This website contains useful information, but some of it is ______________________. (*veraltet*)

8 It's only a ______________________ job, 20 hours a week. (*Teilzeit-*)

9 Fortunately the ______________________ is quite good. (*Lohn*)

10 Are you able to use ______________________? (*Elektrowerkzeuge*)

11 The job ______________________ a clean driving licence. (*erfordert*)

12 I worked as a ______________________ for two years. (*Verkäuferin*)

13 You're ______________________ to get the job without good exam results. (*unwahrscheinlich*)

14 We need to ______________________ why the company ______________________. (*herausfinden, scheiterte*)

15 I like my job because the tasks are ______________________ so it's never boring. (*abwechslungsreich*)

16 The job is really ______________________ – I thought it would be easier. (*anspruchsvoll*)

17 We need to ______________________ why the project went wrong. (*bewerten*)

18 He thought the ______________________ went well and he might get the job. (*Vorstellungsgespräch*)

UNIT 8 Youth crime

according to	According to Bill, the story isn't true.	nach, gemäß, zufolge
to attack	A man attacked him with a knife.	angreifen
to attempt	Don't attempt to run. You won't get far.	versuchen
bald	My dad had lots of hair, but now he's bald.	kahl, glatzköpfig
bank robber	We're bank robbers: give us the money!	Bankräuber/in
beer	Beer and wine are types of alcohol.	Bier
to break	Cheap tools always break after a while.	kaputtgehen
broken	My foot is broken, so I can't run.	gebrochen, kaputt
bully	Leave him alone, you bully!	Mobber/in, Tyrann/in
bullying	Many students experience bullying.	Mobben
to commit (a crime)	They committed 20 crimes before the police found them.	(eine Straftat) begehen
court	We'll find out the truth in court.	Gericht
crime	The police say crime is worse than ever.	Kriminalität; Straftat
curly	Your hair was curly but now it's straight.	lockig
depressed	He's depressed and unhappy.	deprimiert
either ... or	We can play either football or hockey.	entweder ... oder
fine	He must pay a €200 fine.	Geldstrafe
to get in trouble	Careful! You'll get in trouble with the teacher.	Ärger bekommen
glasses	I can't read this without my glasses.	Brille
greedy	You don't need that much, you're greedy.	gierig, habgierig
guilty	Don't lie. You did it. We know you're guilty.	schuldig
honest	I never lie. I'm very honest.	ehrlich
to hurry up	Hurry up! We'll miss the film.	sich beeilen
to hurt sb	Ouch! You hurt me!	jdm wehtun
to ignore	Just ignore him and maybe he'll be quiet.	ignorieren, nicht beachten
innocent	I didn't do it. I'm innocent.	unschuldig

to insult	'You're stupid!' – 'Don't insult me!'	beleidigen, beschimpfen
to involve	This doesn't involve you. Keep out of it!	betreffen
judge	The judge listened to both sides.	Richter/in
jury	There were 12 men and women in the jury.	die Geschworenen
lie	That's a lie! It isn't true.	Lüge
light	He was wearing a light blue jacket.	hell
minority	Only a minority of women like their looks.	Minderheit
nose	Too much alcohol gives you a red nose.	Nase
to pay	It always pays to work hard.	sich auszahlen
to pretend	You heard me. Don't pretend that you didn't.	vorgeben, sich ausgeben als
prison	The judge sent him to prison for two months.	Gefängnis
probation	You'll get two years on probation.	Bewährung
property	That bag isn't your property, it's mine.	Eigentum
punishment	Your punishment is to go to prison.	Bestrafung, Strafe
to repeat	Could you repeat that? I didn't hear you.	wiederholen
to rob	They robbed the old lady and took her bag.	rauben, berauben
to shoplift	If you shoplift, we will call the police.	Ladendiebstahl begehen
shoplifting	Shoplifting costs this shop €1000 every week.	Ladendiebstahl
to steal	Help! He's stealing my car!	stehlen
suicide	He's dead. It was suicide, not murder.	Selbstmord
to survive	She's very sick, but she will survive.	überleben
thief	Stop the thief! He took my money!	Dieb/in
to treat	He treats his girlfriend well.	jdn behandeln
trial	The murder trial lasted for six weeks.	Gerichtsverhandlung
vandalism	Is graffiti vandalism or art?	Vandalismus
victim	The victim had to go to hospital.	Opfer
vote	We had a vote to decide who won.	Abstimmung
witness	She saw it all. She's a witness.	Zeuge/Zeugin
youth	There's nothing wrong with modern youth: we're just young people.	Jugend, Jugendlicher

How much have you learned? Do the tasks to find out.
Only look at pages 36–37 if you are stuck.

1 **Complete the crossword.**

1 It's the opposite of dark.

2 This is when you call someone a nasty name.

3 This is a statement that isn't true.

4 Something that belongs to you is your ... .

5 This is when you want more than you need.

6 If you can't see very well, maybe you need these.

7 This is a word for a young person, or young people in general.

8 A person who doesn't have any hair on their head is ... .

9 This is an illegal action.

10 If you're late for school, you need to ... up.

11 If you say something more than once, you ... it.

2 **Complete the word grid to find out why Sarah is in court.**

1 Sarah won't have to go to SOPNIR because it isn't a serious crime.

2 Her teacher says that Sarah is SETHON. She always tells the truth.

3 This is the first time that she has got into RUBTEOL with the police.

4 Hopefully she won't get a harsh MENHITPUNS.

5 One of Sarah's friends is a LUBLY. She makes the other girls do what she wants.

6 A NISSWET says that Sarah didn't do it.

7 It might be the other girl who is the FETIH.

8 A lot of people SLEAT from this shop. It costs the shop a lot of money.

9 It isn't nice to be the MITCIV of a crime.

10 Sarah says that she is TENINONC, but she won't say who did it.

11 If the court decides that she is LUTGIY, she'll have to pay a large fine.

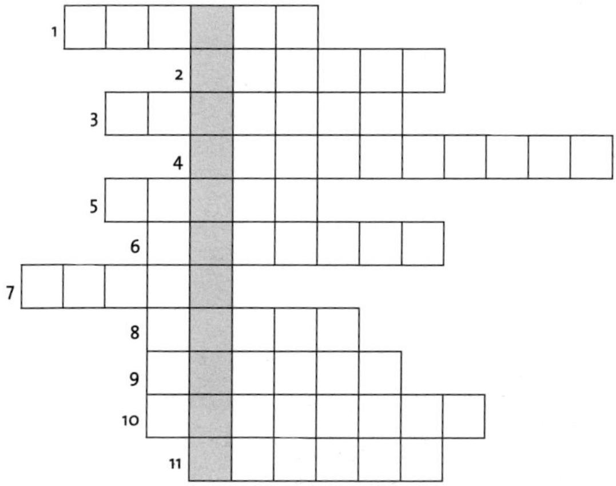

Sarah's crime: ______________________________

UNIT 9 Buying and selling

action	Enough talking! It's time to take action.	Handeln, Aktion
to add up	I've added up the money. We made €15.	zusammenrechnen
to advertise	We'll advertise the job in the newspaper.	bewerben, Werbung machen für
baggy	'This shirt is too baggy.' – 'That's the style.'	weit (geschnitten)
barbecue	The weather's nice. Let's have a barbecue.	Grill(party)
billboard	I saw my face 5 metres high on a billboard.	Werbetafel
buyer	I've found a buyer for my bike. He'll pay €50.	Käufer/in
cable	Is this the cable from the TV?	Kabel
cash	We don't take credit cards, only cash.	bar
cash desk	I want to buy this. Where's the cash desk?	Kasse
changing room	Clothes shops often have a changing room.	Umkleidekabine
to charge (a price)	If you aren't happy with your meal, we won't charge you for it.	(einen Preis) verlangen, berechnen
to clean up	Who's going to clean up after the party?	saubermachen
clerk	The clerk in the store was very helpful.	Verkäufer/in
conclusion	In conclusion, we have seen that ...	Schluss
contract	I signed the contract for my new flat today.	Vertrag
crowd	There was a crowd of about 100 people.	Menge
crowded	This disco is crowded. You can't dance.	überfüllt
to decorate	I always decorate the Christmas tree.	dekorieren
delicious	Mmm! This food is delicious.	lecker
discount	I'll give you a discount if you buy 12 bottles.	Rabatt, Nachlass
effective	It's not very effective – it doesn't work.	effektiv
empty	The bag is empty. There's nothing in it.	leer
to hire sb	He hired waiters to bring the guests food.	jdn beauftragen
host	This is a wonderful party. You're a great host!	Gastgeber/in
introduction	Start your talk with an introduction.	Einleitung

invoice	Don't pay now. I'll send you an invoice.	Rechnung
item of clothing	Buy two items of clothing, get the third free!	Kleidungsstück
to lend	Can you lend me €10? I'll give it back.	leihen
narrow	My street is narrow. There's no room to park.	eng
optional	⚠ Aussprache	optional
to pack	It's time to go. Have you packed your bag?	packen, einpacken
to pass sth	We're lost. We've passed here three times.	an etw vorbeigehen
percentage	What percentage of teenagers use drugs?	Anteil, Prozentsatz
to plug sth in	It won't work unless you plug it in, silly!	etw anschließen, einstecken
to present	She presented the new car at the Motor Show.	vorstellen, präsentieren
presentation	I gave a presentation in front of the class.	Präsentation
prize	I've won a prize! A holiday in Spain!	Preis
to recommend	Can you recommend a good restaurant?	empfehlen
to research	Use the internet to research the answers.	recherchieren
service	Our cleaning service costs €20 an hour.	Dienstleistung
to shop	Do you often shop in this supermarket?	einkaufen
size	What size T-shirt is that, medium or large?	Größe
speaker	There's no music from that speaker.	Lautsprecher
to store	My iPod can store 20,000 songs.	speichern
to suit sb	Green suits you. You should wear it more.	*(Kleider:)* jdm stehen
suitcase	This suitcase is too small for all my clothes.	Koffer
sunglasses	The sun is very bright. I need my sunglasses.	Sonnenbrille
target group	Our target group is teenagers 13–16.	Zielgruppe
tight	This T-shirt is too tight. I can't put it on.	eng
to try sth on	I want to try on this skirt before I buy it.	etw anprobieren
to turn sth on	How do I turn this camera on?	etw anschalten
to type (in)	Type in your name and password.	(ein)tippen
use	I made good use of my French in France.	Gebrauch
waist	I'm fatter than I was. My waist is 95 cm.	Taille

How much have you learned? Do the tasks to find out.
Only look at pages 40–41 if you are stuck.

1 **Find the vowels to complete the missing words.**

1 They cooked steak and burgers on the ______________________ BRBC.
2 Don't forget to finish your essay with a ______________________ CNCLSN.
3 I hate shopping in ______________________ CRWDD stores.
4 This chocolate cake is ______________________ DLCS.
5 The store is offering a 20% ______________________ DSCNT.
6 We haven't paid because we haven't received your ______________________ NVC yet.
7 A large ______________________ PRCNTG of people buy food in the supermarket.
8 The company ______________________ RSRCHD its customers' opinions about the new product.
9 Those clothes don't really ______________________ ST him. They make him look old.
10 We need something more ______________ FFCTV so we can work more quickly.
11 Can you turn the ______________ SPKRS down, please? The music is very loud.

2 **Complete the sentences with the correct prepositions.**

1 Can you add _____ these numbers for me? I think I've made a mistake.
2 My mobile phone is dead. Can I plug it _____ somewhere, please?
3 Why have you turned _____ the TV? We're going out now.
4 We'd better clean _____ this room before Mum and Dad get home.
5 Where can I try _____ this shirt, please?
6 Make sure the website is safe before you type _____ your credit card number.

3 **Find the following words in the word square. Write the German meaning next to each word.**

Two places in a clothing store (two words each):

______________________ ______________________

______________________ ______________________

One person in a store:

______________________ ______________________

Two things you might buy in a big store:

______________________ ______________________

______________________ ______________________

Two things you need to know when you buy clothing:

______________________ ______________________

______________________ ______________________

Two adjectives to describe clothing:

______________________ ______________________

______________________ ______________________

C	A	S	H	D	E	S	K	H	J	A	R
H	R	E	A	B	E	U	G	M	U	R	C
A	A	B	F	I	R	I	T	A	S	Y	L
N	L	A	A	O	L	T	B	E	I	L	E
G	E	G	R	K	E	C	U	S	Z	F	R
I	R	G	G	E	R	A	R	N	E	T	K
N	G	Y	W	A	I	S	T	U	O	I	M
G	J	W	J	R	A	E	H	W	I	G	I
R	O	H	K	A	I	A	I	R	O	H	N
O	U	A	E	T	Y	W	S	K	E	T	Q
O	S	U	N	G	L	A	S	S	E	S	A
M	T	T	A	R	I	R	L	Y	S	Y	R

Unit 10 In and around the office

almost	She's almost 17. Her birthday is next week.	fast, beinah
amusement	Disneyland is an amusement park.	Vergnügung
animated film	It isn't an animated film. It has live actors.	Zeichentrickfilm
to auction (off)	He auctioned off the things he didn't want.	versteigern
auction	She paid €5 for the bag in an eBay auction.	Versteigerung
box office	The film was a success at the box office.	(Theater-, Kino-) Kasse
branch	I work in the Berlin branch of the company.	Zweig, Sparte
breakthrough	He was 45 when he had his breakthrough.	Durchbruch
brochure	This brochure tells you about the company.	Prospekt, Werbebroschüre
caller	Someone phoned. The caller's name was Sid.	Anrufer/in
conference	200 business people were at the conference.	Konferenz
corporation	Microsoft is a very large corporation.	Konzern, Gesellschaft
creation	The creation of the world took seven days.	Schöpfung
creator	J.K. Rowling was the creator of Harry Potter.	Schöpfer/in
drawer	The diary is in the top drawer of my desk.	Schublade
to earn	I earn €500 a week in my job.	verdienen, einspielen
envelope	I need an envelope for this letter.	Briefumschlag
to figure out	Can you figure out the answer?	herausfinden
finance	⚠ Aussprache	Finanz-
firm	Our firm sells computer systems.	Firma
floor	He works on the fourth floor of the building.	Stockwerk, Etage
gardener	She pays a gardener to look after her garden.	Gärtner/in
genius	Einstein was a genius.	Genie
to get rid of sth	Get rid of those books. You don't need them.	etw loswerden
gigantic	King Kong is a film about a gigantic gorilla.	riesig
to greet sb	Who will greet the Queen when she arrives?	jdn begrüßen
half, halves	Somebody has eaten half of this cake.	Hälfte, Hälften

intern	I'm an intern, so they don't pay me to work.	Praktikant/in
inventor	Diesel was the inventor of the diesel engine.	Erfinder/in
to join	Would you like to join our club?	beitreten, mitmachen
keyboard	This computer doesn't have a keyboard.	Tastatur
label	The address is on the label.	Etikett
length	Four hours? There aren't many films of that length.	Länge
mail	Do you get a lot of mail from fans?	Post
mail room	Take these letters to the mail room.	Poststelle
to move	The family moved from Berlin to Munich.	umziehen
package	Please take this package to the post office.	Paket
producer	She works as a film producer in Hollywood.	Produzent/in
production	Production of the new car will start in January next year.	Produktion, Herstellung
publisher	'Who is the book's publisher?' – 'Cornelsen.'	Verleger/in, Verlag
to put sb through	I'll put you through to Mr Jones now.	*(Telefon:)* jdn durchstellen
puzzle	There is a difficult puzzle in this magazine.	Rätsel
to realise sth	Few people are able to realise their dreams.	etw verwirklichen
reception	Please go to reception first.	Empfang, Rezeption
receptionist	The receptionist will show you to my office.	Empfangs-mitarbeiter/in
resort	We're going to a holiday resort in Spain.	Urlaubsort
secretary	I'm his secretary. Sorry, he's not here now.	Sekretär/in
sensation	⚠ Aussprache	Sensation
shelf, shelves	There were ten books on the shelf.	Regal, Regale
shocked	I was shocked to hear that news story.	schockiert
to sort	Please sort these T-shirts into groups.	sortieren
to specialize in sth	We specialize in design: that's all we do.	sich auf etw spezialisieren
successful	It was successful and made lots of money.	erfolgreich
to work overtime	I have to work overtime this weekend.	Überstunden machen

How much have you learned? Do the tasks to find out.
Only look at pages 44–45 if you are stuck.

1 **Complete the puzzle to find the name of a large company. What does it make and which country is it based in?**

1 Please put the magazines on those LEVHESS.

2 I need to send this letter. Where are the LEONEPSEV?

3 Print the customer's address on a BALLE.

4 How do I get an Umlaut on this American DEOKARBY?

5 If you want to see her, you'll have to call her SERTYRACE.

6 There are some pens in the REDAWR of my desk.

7 Is there any LIMA for me today?

8 Where can I leave this KAPAGEC?

9 Ask the lady at NOERETPIC, just inside the main door.

10 He ESRAN about €2000 a month.

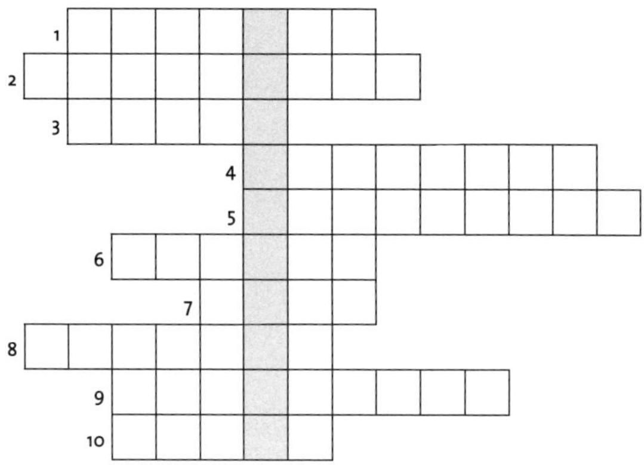

Main product: ______________________________

Country: ______________________________

2 **Complete the sentences with the English translations of the words in brackets.**

1 How long have you worked for the ______________________________ ? (*Firma*)

2 Mr Brennan's office is on the third ______________________________ . (*Etage*)

3 This ______________________________ is about our apprenticeship programme. (*Broschüre*)

4 Did the ______________________________ leave her name? (*Anruferin*)

5 It's ______________________________ five o'clock. (*fast*)

6 How much ______________________________ will I have to work? (*Überstunden*)

7 The company ______________________________ from Paris to Salzburg last year. (*umziehen*)

8 Are any of the world's largest ______________________________ German? (*Konzerne*)

9 What does it take to be ______________________________ in business? (*erfolgreich*)

10 I'll just ________________ you ________________ to the personnel manager. (*durchstellen*)

11 How can we ______________________________ all this rubbish? (*loswerden*)

12 I can't ______________________________ how to use this software. (*herausfinden*)

13 ______________________________ should ______________________________ visitors to the company politely. (*Empfangsmitarbeiter/innen, begrüßen*)

14 Can the ______________________________ go to the sales meeting in New York? (*Praktikanten/innen*)

15 The company has over 200 ______________________________ across the world. (*Zweige*)

16 Our office is on the top ______________________________ of the building. (*Stockwerk*)

17 The Munich office ______________________________ web design. (*sich spezialisiert auf*)

18 I need to go to the ______________________________ to pick up a ______________________________ . (*Poststelle, Paket*)

19 When the firm closed, they ______________________________ off all their office furniture. (*versteigern*)

20 This year's ______________________________ will be in Hamburg. (*Konferenz*)

Unit 11 Our environment

to aim	We aim to change the world.	beabsichtigen
appearance	Can you describe the man's appearance?	Aussehen
at first	It was difficult at first, but it became easier.	zunächst
back	Can you take this heavy box? My back hurts.	Rücken
bright	That's a bright T-shirt! I need my sunglasses!	*(Farbe:)* leuchtend
brilliant	A party? What a brilliant idea!	toll, super
to care about sth	I don't care about that, it isn't my problem.	sich um etw kümmern, scheren
carton	A carton of milk, please.	Karton
community	We are all part of a community.	Gemeinde
to contain	Does this bread contain salt?	enthalten
council	He phoned the council about his neighbours.	Stadtrat, Bezirksrat
damage	Vandals often do a lot of damage.	Schaden
deposit	There's a deposit on this bottle.	Pfand
educational	It isn't just a holiday: it's educational too.	Ausbildungs-
engine	= motor	Motor
to enter	Enter your email address, then click 'Next'.	*(Computer:)* eingeben
environment	The Greens want to help the environment.	Umwelt
environmental	Greenpeace is an environmental group.	Umwelt-
to feel	I don't feel that this is a good idea.	glauben, der Ansicht sein
gang	Teenage gangs are a problem in some towns.	Bande
to garden	She likes to garden in her free time.	gärtnern
gloves	My hands are warm in these gloves.	Handschuhe
goods	We'll send you the goods within 14 days.	Ware(n)
to grow sth	She grows vegetables in her garden.	etw anbauen
height	My height is 1.67 metres.	Höhe
housing estate	We live on a housing estate with 500 houses.	Wohnsiedlung

leaflet	Read this leaflet about the environment.	Flugblatt
litter	It is forbidden to drop litter on the street.	Abfall
local	I'm not local. I'm just here on holiday.	örtlich, ansässig
lonely	Aren't you lonely, living here by yourself?	einsam
natural	Wood is a natural material.	natürlich
nowadays	Once kids were polite. Nowadays they aren't.	heutzutage, jetzt
order	I'd like to make an order for 50 books, please.	Auftrag, Bestellung
organic	Organic farms don't use chemicals.	Bio-
to prevent	Can we prevent this problem in the future?	verhindern
process	The computer processes the data quickly.	bearbeiten
to protect	We need to protect nature.	schützen
rather than	Let's have chips rather than salad.	statt
recyclable	Glass bottles are recyclable.	recyclebar
to relax	Relax! It's time to stop work.	sich entspannen, sich erholen
to remove	Remove your hat when you enter the church.	entfernen
roof	Put a roof on to keep the rain and snow out.	Dach
rubbish	We can't use this. It's just rubbish.	Müll, Abfall
to select	Select the ones that you want.	(aus)wählen
space	It's small. There isn't space for 50 people.	Platz
supplier	We get these paints from a special supplier.	Lieferant, Anbieter
surroundings	We live in beautiful surroundings by the sea.	Umgebung
sweets	Young children eat too many sweets.	Süßigkeiten
tidy	His room is always tidy.	sauber
urban	I live in an urban area, not in the country.	städtisch, Stadt-
to value	He values time with his family.	schätzen
vandal	Vandals broke the glass.	Vandale
to vandalize	Hey! Don't vandalize that bus stop!	verwüsten
to wake up	Wake up! It's almost 9 o'clock.	aufwachen
wall	Why don't we put a picture on the wall?	Wand, Mauer
wildlife	You can see the wildlife if you are quiet.	Tierwelt

How much have you learned? Do the tasks to find out.
Only look at pages 48–49 if you are stuck.

1 **Read the clues and complete the words.**

1 This is how you look.
ap ______________________

2 This is a group of people who live in the same area.
co ______________________

3 It's another way of saying 'have inside'.
co ______________________

4 If you learn something from an activity, it's this.
ed ______________________

5 This is the natural world.
en ______________________

6 This adjective means 'about/of the natural world'.
en ______________________

7 A company gets this from its customers.
or ______________________

8 If you see this on a label, the product is made only from natural things.
or ______________________

9 You do this when you make sure something doesn't happen.
pre ______________________

10 You do this to something when you keep it safe.
pro ______________________

11 If materials can be used again, they're this.
re ______________________

12 It's what you do when you don't need to worry.
re ______________________

13 You do this to something when you take it away.
re ______________________

14 This is a company that sells goods to another company.
sup ______________________

15 They're around you.
sur ______________________

2 Complete the crossword.

1 einsam
2 heutzutage
3 Bande
4 toll, super
5 leuchtend
6 sauber
7 Ware(n)
8 Süßigkeiten
9 Wand, Mauer
10 städtisch
11 Abfall
12 örtlich

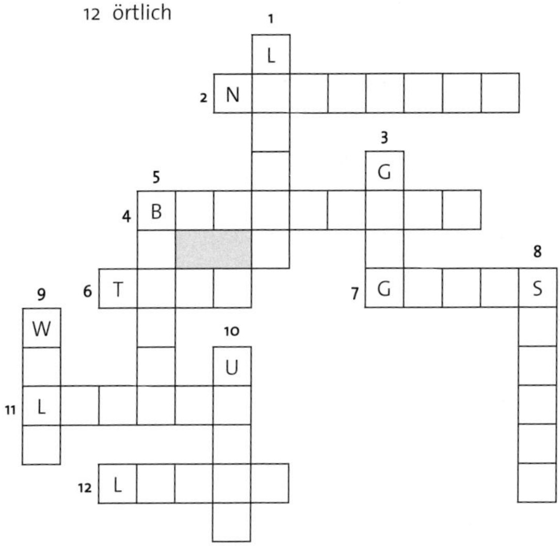

3 Complete the sentences with the missing words.

1 I always wake _____ at 7 o'clock to go to school.

2 I put a deposit _____ a new flat.

3 He really cares _____ his friends and family.

4 He was quiet _____ first, but now he's really loud.

5 The organisation aims _____ help people with no money.

UNIT 12 The right job for me?

academic	She works at the university as an academic.	Akademiker/in
adolescence	Adolescence can be difficult for teenagers.	Jugend, Pubertät
adulthood	When we reach adulthood, we'll get a job.	Erwachsenenalter
analytical	Analytical people like to solve problems.	analytisch
astrological sign	There are 12 astrological signs in the zodiac.	Sternzeichen
bartender	Bartender! Another beer, please.	Barkeeper
characteristic	⚠ Aussprache	Merkmal, Eigenschaft
to chase	That dog always chases cats.	jagen, nachjagen
childhood	Did you have a happy childhood?	Kindheit
clue	Who did it? This could be a clue.	Hinweis
communicative	He isn't communicative. He doesn't talk.	kommunikativ
determined	I'm determined to do it. Don't try to stop me.	entschlossen
to die	We know that we're all going to die one day.	sterben
diploma	You need a diploma to do this job.	Abschluss
to divorce	They divorced and found new partners.	sich scheiden lassen
to drop out (of school)	He dropped out of school and got a job.	(die Schule) abbrechen
drop-out	I'm not a drop-out, I'm just taking a year off.	(Schul-, Uni-) Abbrecher/in
emotional	⚠ Aussprache	emotional
to fall in love	He fell in love with his friend's girlfriend.	sich verlieben
to fill an order	We can't fill the order. We have no goods.	einen Auftrag ausführen
flavour	'What flavour is your ice-cream?' – 'Banana.'	Geschmack, Aroma
generous	'Here's €100.' – 'That's very generous of you.'	großzügig
happiness	Isn't happiness more important than money?	Glück
humorous	It's a humorous story: it makes people laugh.	witzig, humorvoll
to imitate	Don't imitate the teacher, she'll see you!	imitieren, nachmachen

lightning	There was a lot of lightning during the storm.	Blitz
to manage	It was difficult, but she managed to do it.	gelingen, es schaffen
miserable	You look miserable. Is something wrong?	elend
to neglect	Don't neglect your schoolwork.	vernachlässigen
nervous	She's nervous about her exams.	nervös
nurse	The nurse gave the patient some pills.	Krankenschwester, Krankenpfleger
precision	You need precision to make small machines.	Präzision, Präzisions-
profession	It isn't just a job, it's a profession.	Beruf
quality	Is the quality of the photo high enough?	Qualität
to quit school	She quit school before her exams.	die Schule schmeißen
rebellious	She's rebellious. She never does what I want.	rebellisch
to reduce	You'll have to reduce the size of the photo.	verringern, mindern
romance	Paris is a great city for romance.	Romanze
to save sb	Save me! I can't swim!	jdn retten
to scare sb	The mouse scared the elephant.	jdn erschrecken, jdm Angst machen
sensitive	Don't be so sensitive. It was just a joke.	sensibel
to separate	They've separated, but they're not divorced.	(sich) trennen
to share	You can share this sandwich with me.	teilen
to shoot	They shot the film in New Zealand.	*(Film:)* drehen
shot	This next shot was taken later in the day.	*(Film:)* Einstellung, Szene
to slow sth down	Downloading films slows down my internet connection.	etw verlangsamen, bremsen
to strike	A piece of glass struck him on the arm.	treffen
to study	He studied languages at university.	lernen, studieren
therefore	There's no bus, therefore we must walk.	deshalb, daher
unpredictable	The weather's unpredictable. It could rain.	unberechenbar
viewer	Viewers under 12 should not watch this film.	Zuschauer/in
wide	How wide is your TV screen?	breit, weit, groß

How much have you learned? Do the tasks to find out.
Only look at pages 52–53 if you are stuck.

1 **Find the following words in the word square. Write the German meaning next to each word.**

Three stages in a person's life:

Eight adjectives describing personal characteristics:

Two emotions or feelings:

G	R	A	R	M	N	I	P	G	R	Y	R	Y
U	A	D	O	L	E	S	C	E	N	C	E	R
R	D	D	M	L	R	P	O	N	A	K	B	M
T	U	R	A	Y	V	O	R	E	E	R	E	I
M	L	A	N	H	O	S	M	R	R	O	L	S
A	T	E	C	U	U	S	I	O	B	O	L	E
R	H	F	E	M	S	I	C	U	U	B	I	R
D	O	J	R	O	P	T	A	S	F	U	O	A
I	O	K	K	R	A	Y	N	H	A	P	U	B
S	D	E	U	O	R	A	O	Y	P	O	S	L
C	O	M	M	U	N	I	C	A	T	I	V	E
R	S	E	N	S	I	T	I	V	E	N	E	S
A	C	H	I	L	D	H	O	O	D	I	T	Y
N	E	O	D	E	T	E	R	M	I	N	E	D
H	A	P	P	I	N	E	S	S	O	C	T	Y

2 Work out the anagrams to complete the sentences.

1 Twenty per cent of couples ______________________ RECDOVI within five years.

2 Do you think that organic food has a better ______________________ LOURAFV?

3 Our TV was damaged when ______________________ HLINGTING struck the power lines.

4 We looked for Chloe everywhere, but we didn't ______________________ NAGAME to find her.

5 When he fell in love with Ruby, Jack ______________________ GECLENDET his friends.

6 I prefer to play golf as a hobby, I don't want to make it my ______________________ SIFONEPSRO.

7 How can we ______________________ EDREUC the number of people who die on our roads?

8 When parents ______________________ REETASPA, it's usually difficult for the children.

9 It may seem like a good idea, but the results would be ______________________ DENRIPETACLUB.

10 The programme was watched by four million ______________________ SIVEWRE.

11 Barry had to work hard to get his ______________________ PAMOILD.

12 My ______________________ GACSORILTAOL sign is Pisces, but I don't believe in all that stuff.

13 It was late, ______________________ HREOTEFER I left.

14 I had to go to the ______________________ RUNES to get some medicine.

15 She was ______________________ IEAEMRSBL when she moved to Hamburg and had no friends.

16 She was ______________________ ROENUVS when she started her new school.

UNIT 13 Working in Europe

administrative	I have an administrative job, in the office.	Verwaltungs-
to afford sth	Can we afford it, or is it too expensive?	sich etw leisten können
ambitious	I'm ambitious: I want a better job.	ehrgeizig
to be/go short of sth	I'm short of money. Could you give me €50?	nicht genug von etw haben
border	This is the border between France and Italy.	Grenze
to break sth	Sorry! I've just broken a glass.	etw kaputtmachen
broad	<> narrow	breit, groß
builder	He's a builder. He builds houses.	Bauarbeiter/in
capital	Berlin is the capital of Germany.	Hauptstadt
to cause	Bad weather caused the train to be late.	verursachen
cold	You'll get a cold if you go out in a T-shirt.	Erkältung
to confirm	Ask the teacher to confirm if it's right.	bestätigen
data entry	You can't make mistakes in a data entry job.	Dateneingabe
dental assistant	The dental assistant will clean your teeth.	Zahnmedizinische/r Fachangestellte/r
dentist	A dentist works with people's teeth.	Zahnarzt/-ärztin
difficulty	I'm having difficulty with this. It's hard.	Schwierigkeit
emergency	It's an emergency. Phone the police!	Notfall
examination	Please take off your shirt for the examination.	Untersuchung
to fetch	Please fetch the next patient.	holen
file	All your information is in the file.	(Patienten-)Akte
to fill in	Fill in your name and address, please.	ausfüllen
flag	That's the German flag on the Reichstag.	Flagge
form	The form contains a lot of information.	Formular
to get casual jobs	We can get casual jobs as waiters.	jobben
to hand	Please hand me the photo.	überreichen
health care	I would like to work in health care.	Gesundheitswesen

hostel	It's fun to stay in a hostel on holiday.	(Jugend-)Herberge
job opportunity	I'm looking for a job opportunity in sales.	offene Stelle
laboratory	The laboratory will test the blood.	Labor
lift	Can I get a lift to Stuttgart in your car?	Mitfahrgelegenheit
medical assistant	A medical assistant helps a doctor.	Medizinische/r Fachangestellte/r
misunder-standing	It was a misunderstanding. I know now.	Missverständnis
to paraphrase	I don't understand. Could you paraphrase?	umschreiben
to pass	Can you pass me the bottle of water, please?	reichen, geben
patient	⚠ Aussprache	Patient/in
to persuade sb	I'm going. Don't try to persuade me to stay.	jdn überzeugen, überreden
practice	How many doctors work at this practice?	Praxis
range	He has tried a range of different jobs.	Spannbreite
resource	⚠ Aussprache	Mittel, Ressource
to realize	I didn't realize that you were German.	bemerken
to require	I'm fine. I don't require any help, thanks.	verlangen
to return	= go back	zurückkehren
rather	I would rather work in a big company.	eher
to run out of sth	We can't buy it: we've run out of money.	etw nicht mehr haben
to settle down	I want to see the world before I settle down.	sesshaft werden
surgery	It's a small surgery with two doctors.	Arztpraxis
to swipe (a chip card)	I need to swipe your card to see your details on the computer.	(eine Chipkarte) durchziehen
thoroughness	Thoroughness is important: forget nothing!	Gründlichkeit
treatment	How much will the treatment cost?	Behandlung
to turn sth off	Turn off the TV if you aren't watching it.	etw ausschalten
waiting room	There are 10 people in the waiting room.	Wartezimmer
ward	There are 20 patients in this hospital ward.	(Kranken-)Station
X-ray	His hand may be broken. He needs an X-ray.	Röntgen

How much have you learned? Do the tasks to find out.
Only look at pages 56–57 if you are stuck.

1 **One word doesn't belong. Which one? Translate it into German.**

1 Only phone the hospital if there is a medical ... .
- ☐ emergency
- ☐ misunderstanding
- ☐ difficulty ______________________

2 Nurse, Mrs Jones needs ... .
- ☐ an examination
- ☐ an X-ray
- ☐ a cold ______________________

3 Cathy, could you get me Mr Baker's ... , please?
- ☐ form
- ☐ flag
- ☐ file ______________________

4 Sally Smith? The ... will see you now. Please go through.
- ☐ patient
- ☐ dentist
- ☐ medical assistant ______________________

5 Dr Arnold works in a small ... in the city centre.
- ☐ hostel
- ☐ practice
- ☐ surgery ______________________

6 It was a busy day. There were a lot of sick people in the ... .
- ☐ waiting room
- ☐ ward
- ☐ laboratory ______________________

7 Mr Beasley ... his chip card to the doctor's receptionist.
- ☐ swiped
- ☐ passed
- ☐ handed ______________________

2 **Find the vowels to complete the missing words.**

1 I'm not very ______________________ MBTS. I'm quite happy in this job.

2 ______________________ THRGHNSS is very important when you're cleaning the hospital wards.

3 It's just a ______________________ CSL job for a few months.

4 Is the ______________________ HLTH ______________________ CR system in the UK different to ours in Germany?

5 Luckily, Jack didn't ______________________ BRK his arm when he fell off the wall.

6 Junk food and little exercise ______________________ CS many medical problems.

7 Please can you ______________________ CNFRM your date of birth?

8 If you give the card to me, I'll ______________________ SWP it for you.

9 We ______________________ RQR someone who can start work next week.

10 The careers adviser ______________________ PRSDD Michael to apply for a job as a dental assistant.

11 When did you ______________________ RLZ that you were ill?

12 The ______________________ TRTMNT for this problem is very expensive, Mrs Wilson. Can you afford it?

13 What will we do if all the foreign nurses ______________________ RTRN home?

14 In my job I have a ______________________ BRD ______________________ RNG of administrative tasks.

15 Are you having ______________________ DFFCLTY with the form? I'll help you fill it in.

16 I've found a good job ______________________ PPRTNTY in a hospital in England.

17 I work in a large ______________________ SRGRY in the city. We have ten doctors.

UNIT 14 It's an emergency!

ambulance	I think she's broken her leg. Call an ambulance.	Krankenwagen, Rettungswagen
to arrest sb	The police arrested the criminal.	jdn verhaften
bandage	⚠ Aussprache	Bandage
birth	The birth went well and the baby is OK.	Geburt
to celebrate	Let's have a party to celebrate your birthday.	feiern
circulation	Cold fingers are a sign of bad circulation.	Kreislauf
civil defence	The civil defence workers saved many lives.	Zivilschutz
complication	It should be easy, but there are complications.	Komplikation
condition	He's in a bad condition. He's very ill.	Zustand; Leiden
conscious	Can you hear me? Are you conscious?	bei Bewusstsein
consciousness	I lost consciousness. I don't know anything.	Bewusstsein
to cover	Cover the milk to keep it fresh.	abdecken , bedecken
crossroad(s)	Do I turn or go straight on at the crossroad?	Kreuzung
custom	In English-speaking countries, the custom is to give Christmas presents on 25 December.	Gepflogenheit, Brauch
dizzy	I looked down at the ground and felt dizzy.	schwindlig
electrician	We don't have any power. Call an electrician.	Elektriker/in
to fail a test	He failed the test and had to take it again.	eine Prüfung nicht bestehen
fire brigade	Help! Fire! Call the fire brigade!	Feuerwehr
fire fighter	When the fire fighters came, the fire was big.	Feuerwehrmann/frau
first-aid kit	I've cut my hand. Where's the first-aid kit?	Verbandskasten
flood	After the flood, the whole house was wet.	Hochwasser
to forgive	'I'm sorry.' – 'That's OK. I forgive you.'	verzeihen
germ	There are germs in that dirty water.	Keim
to give birth	She gave birth to a healthy baby girl.	gebären, ein Kind zur Welt bringen
to hit sb	Don't drive so fast. You'll hit someone.	*hier:* jdn anfahren

in case	Take a coat in case the weather is cold.	falls
individual	We're not the same: we're all individuals.	Individuum
injured	'Are you injured?' – 'No, I'm OK.'	verletzt
level	You have a high level of alcohol in your blood.	Niveau
to misuse	Don't misuse the library. If you want to chat, go outside.	missbrauchen, zweckentfremden
motorway	The motorway is quicker than smaller roads.	Autobahn
pain	I didn't feel much pain when I broke my arm.	Schmerz
painkiller	Take two painkillers every eight hours.	Schmerzmittel
to pass a test	If you pass the test, you can drive a car.	eine Prüfung bestehen
passenger	There were 350 passengers on the aircraft.	Passagier/in
patience	You must work harder. I'm losing patience.	Geduld
plaster	I've cut my finger. Do you have a plaster?	Pflaster
power failure	I can't use the TV. We've had a power failure.	Stromausfall
pulse	'Is she dead?' – 'Can you feel a pulse?'	Puls
to put out (a fire)	It was a small fire, so it was easy to put it out.	(ein Feuer) löschen
to rescue	It took hours to rescue everyone from the sea.	retten
rescuer	I want to thank my rescuers for saving me.	Retter/in
to restore	It took 10 hours to restore power to the house.	wiederherstellen
robbery	They took €100,000 in the robbery.	Raub, Raubüberfall
rural	It's a rural area. There aren't many buildings.	ländlich
scissors	I need a pair of scissors to cut this paper.	Schere
stereotype	It's just a stereotype that Italians love pasta.	Klischee
to take a test	You can take a driving test at the age of 18.	eine Prüfung ablegen
therefore	There's no bus, therefore we'll have to walk.	deshalb, daher
tragedy	After another tragedy, four people are dead.	Tragödie
to trap sb	I shut the door and trapped him in the room.	jdn einschließen
via	We can communicate via email.	über, mittels
wound	There was lots of blood from the wound.	Wunde

How much have you learned? Do the tasks to find out.
Only look at pages 60–61 if you are stuck.

1 **Find the following words in the word square. Write the German meaning next to each word.**

Three things you would find in a first-aid kit:

Three emergency services:

Five things you might check for if someone has been hit by a car:

V	I	C	O	N	S	C	I	O	U	S	N	E	S	S
C	P	A	I	N	K	I	L	L	E	R	S	L	I	N
I	K	S	W	U	O	R	U	R	S	Q	B	E	R	T
V	L	S	O	R	S	C	I	S	S	O	R	S	J	E
I	E	R	U	O	R	U	Y	E	R	R	A	S	A	K
L	R	O	N	F	Y	L	E	I	R	J	A	P	R	P
D	A	M	D	E	R	A	M	T	W	H	R	A	S	L
E	D	L	S	Q	A	T	A	H	U	R	L	I	Q	A
F	I	R	E	B	R	I	G	A	D	E	E	N	A	S
E	S	S	R	A	B	O	Y	U	D	T	A	M	O	T
N	N	R	A	R	A	N	P	R	A	P	U	L	S	E
C	Q	E	W	Q	O	K	U	I	N	I	P	O	R	R
E	I	T	A	M	B	U	L	A	N	C	E	T	A	S

2 **Solve the anagrams to complete the crossword.**

1 There was one SEEPNASGR in the car with the driver.

2 The police SARTEDER the driver for drunk driving.

3 It took three hours to CSUREE the two people.

4 She held a party to CEAREBLET passing her test.

5 How long will the CECLENTAIRI need to restore the power?

6 He doesn't look anything like the SYPRETTOEE of a bank robber.

7 The accident happened on the TAWYOMOR.

8 It's a RUALR area. The nearest house is 2 km away.

9 I feel ZYDIZ – can I sit down?

Unit 15 Globalization

to admit	I must admit, I'm not very good at maths.	zugeben
advantage	One advantage is you can use it everywhere.	Vorteil
agency	The CIA is a US intelligence agency.	Agentur
amazing	That is a surprise. In fact, I find it amazing.	erstaunlich
to be based in ...	The British government is based in London.	seinen Sitz in ... haben
to be well off	We used to be poor, but now we're well off.	gut dran sein
beef	Beef is meat from cows.	Rindfleisch
to benefit from sth	Bad luck for them, but we can benefit from it.	von etw profitieren
to boycott	Should we boycott their products?	boykottieren
buzzword	It's a popular buzzword but means nothing.	Schlagwort
by sea	Did you fly or did you go by sea?	auf dem Seeweg
cargo	The ship has a cargo of cocoa and bananas.	Fracht, Ladung
competitive	We won't be competitive with high prices.	konkurrenzfähig
consumer	We're all consumers: we all buy things.	Verbraucher/in
cotton	My T-shirt is made of cotton.	Baumwolle
customs	Why didn't customs find the illegal drugs?	Zoll
decade	Which decade was he born in? The 1980s?	Jahrzehnt
distribution	I work in distribution. I send goods to shops.	Versand
efficient	⚠ Aussprache	effizient
to exist	Elves and dragons don't exist.	existieren
fairness	I'd like to see more fairness in sport.	Gerechtigkeit
fashionable	Is that a new dress? It's very fashionable.	in Mode, modisch
field	The cows are eating grass in the field.	Feld
freight	The train is carrying freight, not passengers.	Fracht
to give a talk	I gave a talk to my class about globalization.	einen Vortrag halten
globalization	Globalization makes all countries the same.	Globalisierung

HGV (heavy goods vehicle)	There were HGVs, buses and cars on the road.	LKW
to inspect	I need to inspect your bags, madam.	überprüfen, kontrollieren
instant(ly)	I can't give you an instant answer.	sofort(ig)
labour	Farm labour can be very hard work.	Arbeit
latest	Have you seen his latest film?	neueste/r/s
law	Murder is against the law, of course.	Gesetz
limited	His skills are limited. He can't do much.	beschränkt
to make a living	She makes a living as a taxi driver.	den Lebensunterhalt verdienen
meanwhile	Jo left for work. Meanwhile, we stayed here.	unterdessen
originally	Originally I had tea, but then I had coffee.	ursprünglich
potential	The potential problem may not happen.	potenziell
power	The US president has a lot of power.	Macht
powerful	Is China more powerful than the USA?	mächtig
profit	⚠ Aussprache	Gewinn, Profit
protest	⚠ Aussprache	Protest
relative	'Do you have relatives there?' – 'My sister.'	Verwandte/r
to shine	The sun is shining. It's a beautiful day.	scheinen
suit	You should wear a suit to the job interview.	Anzug, Kostüm
surprising	The ending was surprising. I didn't expect it.	überraschend
talk	My talk is about Fairtrade.	Vortrag
taste	Dark chocolate has a bitter taste.	Geschmack
trade	I'll buy your bike for €200. That's a fair trade.	Handel
trainers	Alex runs in Nike trainers.	Turnschuhe
to turn up	I don't know where it is, but it will turn up.	auftauchen
unfair	Hey! You've got more than me. It's unfair.	ungerecht
wage	We want a fair wage for a day's work.	Lohn
watch	What's the time? I'm not wearing my watch.	(Armband-)Uhr
wine	Do you prefer white wine or red?	Wein

How much have you learned? Do the tasks to find out.
Only look at pages 64–65 if you are stuck.

1 **Read the clues and find the words. Then complete the puzzle to show a problem which exists in poor countries.**

a) To refuse to buy goods from a company because you disagree with its actions

8

b) An expression that is popular for a short time

9

c) People who buy things for their own use

1

d) Giving equal rights to everyone

3

e) Able to make others do what you want

6

f) Something which helps you

5

g) People in your family

11 4

h) Not expected

10

i) A period of ten years

7

j) Modern and smart

2

1 2 3 4 5 6 7 8 9 10 11

2 **Complete the sentences with the English translations of the words in brackets.**

1 We'll send the goods to you by ______________________________ . (*LKW*)

2 Aren't there ______________________________ to protect child workers? (*Gesetze*)

3 The European Union does a lot of ______________________________ with the USA. (*Handel*)

4 These children work for a low ______________________________ . (*Lohn*)

5 It may take ten days for the goods to get through ______________________________ . (*Zoll*)

6 How do poor farmers ______________________________ from Fairtrade? (*profitieren*)

7 How can we stay ______________________________ when labour is so cheap in India and China? (*konkurrenzfähig*)

8 I must ______________________________ , I don't know much about globalization. (*zugeben*)

9 Mr Ramotswe from Botswana gave a ______________________________ about Africa. (*Vortrag*)

10 Are you going to wear a ______________________________ for the interview? (*Anzug*)

11 I'm ______________________________ from Kenya, but I live in the UK. (*ursprünglich*)

12 ______________________________ , working conditions in the Third World are getting worse. (*unterdessen*)

13 We eat ______________________________ in our house at least once a week. (*Rindfleisch*)

14 These ______________________________ were made by Adidas. (*Turnschuhe*)

15 Our time is ______________________________ . We have to get everything done before Friday. (*beschränkt*)

16 How much ______________________________ did we make with our new coffee product? (*Gewinn*)

17 The results were ______________________________ . I didn't think we would sell so many bananas. (*überraschend*)

Answer key

Let's go!

1 1 adult; 2 company; 3 creative; 4 phrase; 5 skill; 6 salespeople; 7 strength; 8 tool; 9 training; 10 electricity; 11 repair; 12 adventure; 13 criminal; 14 gap

2 1 favourite; 2 translate; 3 advertisement; 4 clever; 5 popular; 6 surprise; 7 information; 8 technology; 9 build; 10 practical; 11 statement; 12 complicated; 13 extremely; 14 industry; 15 professional; 16 members; 17 character

Unit 1 Fitness and sport

1

				1		2								
				C		L					4			
			3	O	V	E	R	W	E	I	G	H	T	
				N		I					Y			
				V		S		5	F	E	M	A	L	E
6	M	A	L	E		U			8					
				R	7	R	O	U	T	I	N	E		
				S		E			R			9		
				A					A			H		
				T		10	O	P	I	N	I	O	N	
				I					N			M		
		11	C	O	L	L	E	G	E			E		
				N					E			L		
												E		
12	I	N	S	T	R	U	C	T	I	O	N	S		
												S		

2 1 meaning; 2 choice; 3 discuss; 4 timetable; 5 responsible; 6 equipment; 7 carefully; 8 appointment; 9 independent; 10 healthy; 11 safety; 12 difference; 13 laugh; 14 several; 15 current; 16 trainee; 17 leisure; 18 belongs

Unit 2 English around the world

1 **a** abroad; **b** foreign; **c** government; **d** soldiers; **e** homesickness; **f** disaster; **g** health; **h** photograph; **i** technicians; **j** exchange; **k** experience; **l** internship;
puzzle: disaster-relief organization

2 **1** exercise; **2** expect; **3** customers; **4** invite; **5** guess; **6** similar; **7** foreigners; **8** miss; **9** sure; **10** subject; **11** colleagues; **12** driving licence; **13** menu; **14** brand

3 **1** engaged; **2** guessed; **3** advice; **4** vegetarian; **5** exchange; **6** experience; **7** disaster; **8** sure

Unit 3 Free-time activities

1 **2** fluent – fließend; **3** urgent – dringend; **4** musician – Musiker/in;
5 education – (Schul-)Bildung; **6** entertainment – Unterhaltung;
7 apply – sich bewerben; **8** accommodation – Unterkunft;
9 include – beinhalten, umfassen; **10** voluntary – freiwillig, ehrenamtlich;
11 nearby – in der Nähe; **12** payment – Zahlung; **13** retail – Einzelhandel;
14 paramedic – Sanitäter/in; **15** disabled – behindert, Behinderten-;
16 attend – in/zu etw gehen; **17** campsite – Campingplatz; **18** survey – Umfrage, Erhebung;
19 piano – Klavier; **20** primary – Grund-

2 **1** fence; **2** camp; **3** cash; **4** meal; **5** chat; **6** stuff; **7** stage; **8** tent; **9** solve; **10** sign;
instrument: piano

P	S	O	L	V	E	I
N	S	I	G	N	C	S
F	C	H	A	T	A	T
E	M	E	A	L	M	U
N	C	A	S	H	P	F
C	A	T	E	N	T	F
E	O	S	T	A	G	E

Unit 4 Life in the big city

1 nouns: seafood – Meeresfrüchte; ingredient – Zutat; dishes – Gerichte, Geschirr; dessert – Nachtisch; cook – Koch/Köchin; chef – Koch/Köchin; bill – Rechnung; appetizer – Appetithappen
verbs: taste – schmecken; order – bestellen

2

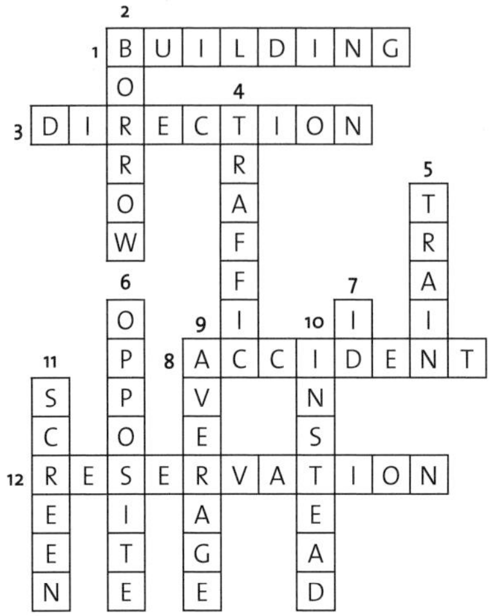

3 1 c; 2 b; 3 e; 4 f; 5 d; 6 a

Unit 5 The world in 2050

1 2 creativity; 3 imagination; 4 invention; 5 speech; 6 thought; 7 waste

2 1 agree; 2 addictive; 3 career; 4 depressing; 5 disagree; 6 employee; 7 hopefully; 8 message; 9 pollution; 10 press; 11 programme; 12 unnecessary

3 1 pensioner; 2 prediction; 3 reason; 4 serious; 5 wealthy; 6 lifetime; 7 compare; 8 unemployment; 9 view; 10 human; 11 optimistic; 12 charity; 13 express; 14 income

Unit 6 Social networks

1 1 comment; 2 embarrassment; 3 explanation; 4 replace; 5 upset; 6 recipient; 7 delete; 8 complain; 9 excellent; 10 invitation; 11 recognize; 12 advise; 13 informal; 14 update; 15 employer

2 nouns to do with communication: network – Netzwerk; noticeboard – Pinnwand; voice – Stimme
verbs you can do to an email: attach – beifügen, anhängen; forward – weiterleiten; receive – erhalten
verbs you can do to a person: apologize – sich entschuldigen; criticize – kritisieren; embarrass – jdm peinlich sein, jdn bloß stellen; hurt – verletzen; offend – beleidigen

N	E	T	W	O	R	K	A	J	A	V
O	F	A	Z	E	O	O	D	S	H	O
T	O	P	U	A	W	H	F	W	H	I
I	F	O	R	W	A	R	D	Y	U	C
C	F	L	U	O	T	E	N	A	R	E
E	E	O	V	G	T	R	E	O	T	A
B	N	G	A	R	A	E	J	I	G	R
O	D	I	R	E	C	E	I	V	E	K
A	R	Z	O	A	H	E	E	R	E	S
R	L	E	M	B	A	R	R	A	S	S
D	C	R	I	T	I	C	I	Z	E	P

Unit 7 Future jobs and training

1

1						M	A	C	H	I	N	E	R	Y	
2				E	M	P	L	O	Y						
3							I	N	T	E	R	V	I	E	W
4				C	L	A	S	S	M	A	T	E	S		
5			P	R	O	M	O	T	I	O	N				
6	E	N	G	I	N	E	E	R							
7			C	A	R	E	F	U	L	L	Y				
8				V	E	H	I	C	L	E	S				
9	M	A	N	U	F	A	C	T	U	R	I	N	G		
10					D	E	C	I	S	I	O	N			
11						K	N	O	W	L	E	D	G	E	
12	P	O	S	I	T	I	O	N							

Amy's choice of industry: construction

2 **1** apprenticeship; **2** button; **3** certain, succeed; **4** install; **5** job-seekers; **6** necessary; **7** out of date; **8** part-time; **9** pay; **10** power tools; **11** requires; **12** sales assistant; **13** unlikely; **14** work out, failed; **15** varied; **16** challenging; **17** evaluate; **18** interview

Unit 8 Youth crime

1

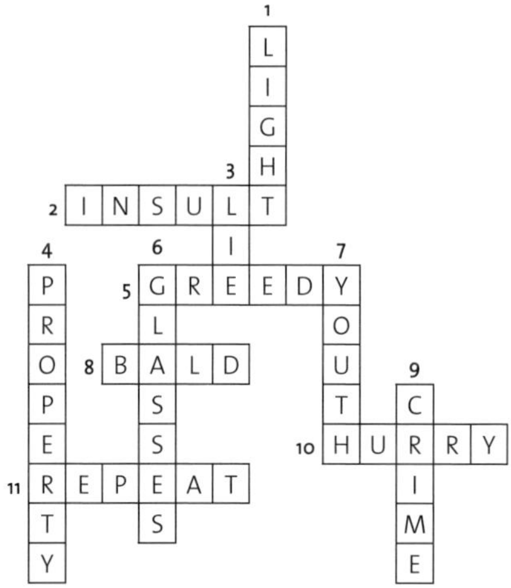

2

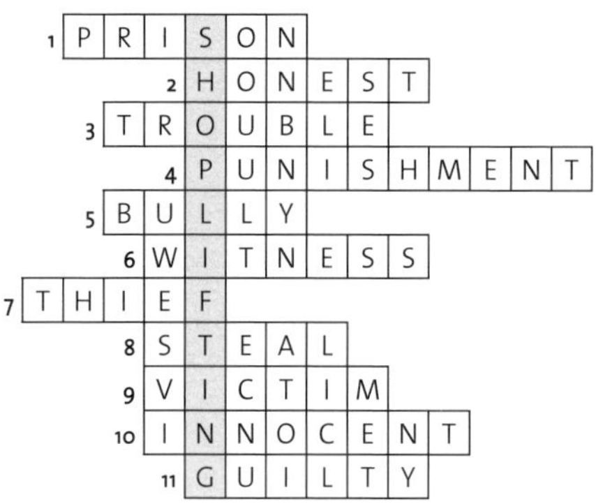

Sarah's crime: shoplifting

Unit 9 Buying and selling

1 **1** barbecue; **2** conclusion; **3** crowded; **4** delicious; **5** discount; **6** invoice; **7** percentage; **8** researched; **9** suit; **10** effective; **11** speakers

2 **1** up; **2** in; **3** on; **4** up; **5** on; **6** in

3 places in a clothing store: cash desk – Kasse; changing room – Umkleidekabine
person in a store: clerk – Verkäufer/in
things you might buy: suitcase – Koffer; sunglasses – Sonnenbrille
things you need to know: size – Größe; waist – Taille
adjectives to describe clothing: baggy – weit (geschnitten); tight – eng

C	A	S	H	D	E	S	K	H	J	A	R
H	R	E	A	B	E	U	G	M	U	R	C
A	A	B	F	I	R	I	T	A	S	Y	L
N	L	A	A	O	L	T	B	E	I	L	E
G	E	G	R	K	E	C	U	S	Z	F	R
I	R	G	G	E	R	A	R	N	E	T	K
N	G	Y	W	A	I	S	T	U	O	I	M
G	J	W	J	R	A	E	H	W	I	G	I
R	O	H	K	A	I	A	I	R	O	H	N
O	U	A	E	T	Y	W	S	K	E	T	Q
O	S	U	N	G	L	A	S	S	E	S	A
M	T	T	A	R	I	R	L	Y	S	Y	R

Unit 10 In and around the office

1

1		S	H	E	L	V	E	S						
2	E	N	V	E	L	O	P	E	S					
3		L	A	B	E	L								
4						K	E	Y	B	O	A	R	D	
5						S	E	C	R	E	T	A	R	Y
6			D	R	A	W	E	R						
7					M	A	I	L						
8	P	A	C	K	A	G	E							
9			R	E	C	E	P	T	I	O	N			
10			E	A	R	N	S							

main product: cars
country: Germany

2 **1** firm; **2** floor; **3** brochure; **4** caller; **5** almost; **6** overtime; **7** moved; **8** corporations; **9** successful; **10** put, through; **11** get rid of; **12** figure out; **13** receptionists, greet; **14** interns; **15** branches; **16** floor; **17** specializes in; **18** mail room, package; **19** auctioned; **20** conference

Unit 11 Our environment

1 **1** appearance; **2** community; **3** contain; **4** educational; **5** environment; **6** environmental; **7** order; **8** organic; **9** prevent; **10** protect; **11** recyclable; **12** relax; **13** remove; **14** supplier; **15** surroundings

2

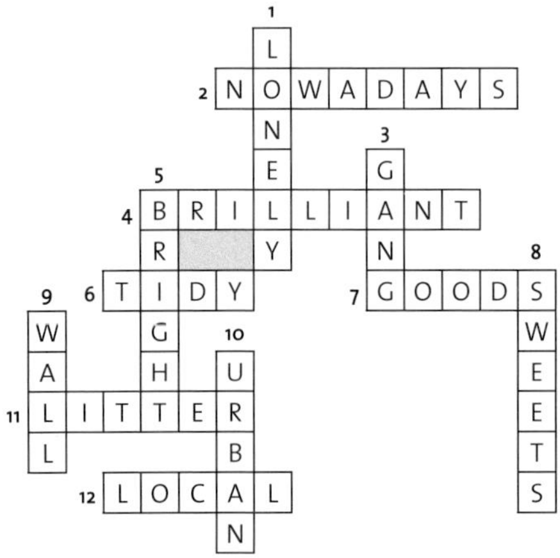

3 **1** up; **2** on; **3** about; **4** at; **5** to

Unit 12 The right job for me?

1 stages in a person's life: adolescence – Jugend, Pubertät; adulthood – Erwachsenenalter; childhood – Kindheit
personal characteristics: communicative – kommunikativ; determined – entschlossen; generous – großzügig; humorous – witzig, humorvoll; miserable – elend; nervous – nervös; rebellious – rebellisch; sensitive – sensible
emotions or feelings: happiness – Glück; romance – Romanze

G	R	A	R	M	N	I	P	G	R	Y	R	Y
U	A	D	O	L	E	S	C	E	N	C	E	R
R	D	D	M	L	R	P	O	N	A	K	B	M
T	U	R	A	Y	V	O	R	E	E	R	E	I
M	L	A	N	H	O	S	M	R	R	O	L	S
A	T	E	C	U	U	S	I	O	B	O	L	E
R	H	F	E	M	S	I	C	U	U	B	I	R
D	O	J	R	O	P	T	A	S	F	U	O	A
I	O	K	K	R	A	Y	N	H	A	P	U	B
S	D	E	U	O	R	A	O	Y	P	O	S	L
C	O	M	M	U	N	I	C	A	T	I	V	E
R	S	E	N	S	I	T	I	V	E	N	E	S
A	C	H	I	L	D	H	O	O	D	I	T	Y
N	E	O	D	E	T	E	R	M	I	N	E	D
H	A	P	P	I	N	E	S	S	O	C	T	Y

2 **1** divorce; **2** flavour; **3** lightning; **4** manage; **5** neglected; **6** profession; **7** reduce; **8** separate; **9** unpredictable; **10** viewers; **11** diploma; **12** astrological; **13** therefore; **14** nurse; **15** miserable; **16** nervous

Unit 13 Working in Europe

1 **1** misunderstanding – Missverständnis; **2** a cold – Erkältung; **3** flag – Flagge; **4** patient – Patient/in; **5** hostel – (Jugend-)Herberge; **6** laboratory – Labor; **7** swiped – durchziehen

2 **1** ambitious; **2** thoroughness; **3** casual; **4** health, care; **5** break; **6** cause; **7** confirm; **8** swipe; **9** require; **10** persuaded; **11** realize; **12** treatment; **13** return; **14** broad, range; **15** difficulty; **16** opportunity; **17** surgery

Unit 14 It's an emergency!

1 things in a first-aid kit: painkillers – Schmerzmittel; plasters – Pflaster; scissors – Schere
emergency services: ambulance – Krankenwagen, Rettungswagen;
civil defence – Zivilschutz; fire brigade – Feuerwehr
things you might check for if someone has been hit by a car: circulation – Kreislauf;
consciousness – Bewusstsein; pain – Schmerz; pulse – Puls; wounds – Wunde

V	I	C	O	N	S	C	I	O	U	S	N	E	S	S
C	P	A	I	N	K	I	L	L	E	R	S	L	I	N
I	K	S	W	U	O	R	U	R	S	Q	B	E	R	T
V	L	S	O	R	S	C	I	S	S	O	R	S	J	E
I	E	R	U	O	R	U	Y	E	R	R	A	S	A	K
L	R	O	N	F	Y	L	E	I	R	J	A	P	R	P
D	A	M	D	E	R	A	M	T	W	H	R	A	S	L
E	D	L	S	Q	A	T	A	H	U	R	L	I	Q	A
F	I	R	E	B	R	I	G	A	D	E	E	N	A	S
E	S	S	R	A	B	O	Y	U	D	T	A	M	O	T
N	N	R	A	R	A	N	P	R	A	P	U	L	S	E
C	Q	E	W	Q	O	K	U	I	N	I	P	O	R	R
E	I	T	A	M	B	U	L	A	N	C	E	T	A	S

2

					1 P	2 A	S	S	E	N	G	E	3 R
						R							E
	4 C	5 E	L	E	B	R	A	T	E				S
		L				E							C
6 S		E				S							U
T		C		7 M	O	T	O	R	W	A	Y		E
E		T				E							
8 R	U	R	A	L		9 D	I	Z	Z	Y			
E		I											
O		C											
T		I											
Y		A											
P		N											
E													

Unit 15 Globalization

1 **a** boycott; **b** buzzword; **c** consumers; **d** fairness; **e** powerful; **f** advantage; **g** relatives; **h** surprising; **i** decade; **j** fashionable;
problem: child labour

2 **1** HGV; **2** laws; **3** trade; **4** wage; **5** customs; **6** benefit; **7** competitive; **8** admit; **9** talk; **10** suit; **11** originally; **12** meanwhile; **13** beef; **14** trainers; **15** limited; **16** profit; **17** surprising